THE   BOOK   OF

GREEK
COOKING

T H E B O O K O F

GREEK
COOKING

LESLEY MACKLEY

Photographed by
JON STEWART

HPBooks
a division of
PRICE STERN SLOAN
Los Angeles

ANOTHER BEST SELLING VOLUME FROM HPBOOKS

HPBooks
A division of Price Stern Sloan, Inc.
11150 Olympic Boulevard
Suite 650
Los Angeles, California 90064

9 8 7 6 5 4 3 2 1

ISBN 1-55788-06-X

By arrangement with Salamander Books Ltd.

Home Economists: Kerenza Harries and Jo Craig
Printed in Belgium by Proost International Book Production

INTRODUCTION

The custom of serving small snacks with drinks is widespread throughout the Mediterranean countries. In Greece, these snacks or mezes can take the form of anything from small nibbles such as olives or pickled peppers served with a glass of ouzo, to a selection of different dishes which make up a more substantial meal.

The first section of this book contains a wide variety of dishes for serving as mezes, but many of the other recipes could be served in smaller quantities as part of a meze selection. Similarly, many of the meze recipes could be increased to make an appetizer, main course, or vegetable accompaniment.

With over 100 beautifully illustrated recipes, this book brings you the full range and variety of Greek cooking, something not always apparent to the casual visitor. There are dishes for every occasion— for entertaining, family meals, buffets and cocktail parties—plus a whole selection of recipes suitable for vegetarians. Some are familiar favorites (sometimes adapted for modern tastes) and others may be less well known, but all are guaranteed to put a little Mediterranean sunshine into your menus!

GREEK COOKING

Greek food is simple, colorful and packed with robust flavors. Although many dishes show influences from Greece's past, particularly Arab, Turkish and Italian, they have a distinctive style of their own; a style which has changed little over the years. Greece has a long tradition of fine cooking and the full range of delicious Greek dishes often remains undiscovered by the tourist.

THE GREEK DIET
The Greek diet, like that of other countries around the Mediterranean, is extremely healthy, being low in processed foods and animal fats, and is based on the availability of local produce: wheat products such as bread, pastry and pasta, fresh fruit and vegetables, fish and olive oil.

MEAT
Meat does not have the significance it has in America as it has always been a comparative luxury. Greece does not have the lush pastures needed to support large herds of cattle, but both sheep and goats can survive on quite poor land.

These hardy animals produce somewhat tougher and better flavored meat than we are used to, but the Greeks make imaginative use of it in recipes which make a small amount of meat stretch a long way. Stews are given long slow cooking until the meat is beautifully tender, and many recipes require the meat to be marinated before cooking which also helps to tenderize it. Little beef is eaten and it is usually cut into cubes for kabobs or ground.

No part of the animal is wasted and offal is used imaginatively in many recipes. For festivals and special occasions, a whole lamb will be rubbed with olive oil, stuffed with herbs and roasted on a spit over a charcoal filled pit, filling the air with the aroma of woodsmoke, herbs and roasting meat.

Traditional Greek recipes give cooking times for meat which result in it practically falling apart, therefore the cooking times given in this book have taken into account the better quality of the meat which will be used.

POULTRY
The first mention of poultry keeping in Europe is in a Greek reference in 570 B.C. and chicken and other poultry,

and game, are as popular as ever. Guinea fowl, partridge and quail all appear in many traditional recipes.

DAIRY PRODUCE
Sheep and goats are traditionally the main dairy animals in Greece, but nowadays much of the milk used is cows' milk. Milk is not used much as a drink mainly because, in the days before refrigeration, it did not keep in the warm climate and had to be made into a longer lasting product such as cheese or yogurt.

Cows', goats' and sheeps' milk are all made into cheeses and yogurts. Sheeps' milk contains more fat and protein than cows' or goats' milk and makes a particularly thick rich yogurt and some excellent cheeses.

Traditionally, butter is not used much in Greek cooking as olive oil is favored as a cooking medium, giving a distinctive Mediterranean flavor to many dishes.

FISH
As the Greek mainland is almost surrounded by sea and much of the country is made up of hundreds of islands, fish naturally plays a very important part in the diet.

The seas are rich with a wide variety of fish all the year round. Red and gray mullet are very popular and turbot, bass, sea bream, swordfish and halibut are also widely used.

Octopus is beaten against the stones on the beach to tenderize it, then it is fried, grilled or cooked in a sauce, as is squid. Crab, mussels, shrimp and lobster are also excellent.

The most popular method of cooking fish is broiling, but it is also frequently cooked in a tomato sauce. Taramasalta is made from smoked fish roe. Originally the roe of the gray mullet was used, but nowadays it is more likely to be cod's roe. Fish soups are popular; it is thought that the well-known Provencal bouillabaisse developed from the Greek kakavia.

VEGETABLES
Vegetables grow well in the sunny climate and are a very important part of the Greek diet. Vegetables are not necessarily considered an accompaniment to meat, but feature in special dishes on their own, or in combinations.

As in all the Mediterranean countries, peppers, tomatoes, zucchini, eggplants, onions and garlic grow in abundance and feature in many recipes but other popular vegetables include horta (similar to spinach), spinach, artichokes, broad beans, green beans, cabbage, fennel, leeks and okra.

Many beans are dried for use in the winter, broad beans, chickpeas, haricot beans and kidney beans being among the most widely used. They are soaked, then cooked, sometimes with other vegetables or in a tomato sauce, or they may be made into a puree or dip, or used in a salad, often combined in a three-bean salad.

FRUIT

Fruit also grows in abundance in the hot sunny climate and market stalls are piled with an enormous variety. Citrus fruits grow well and lemons are particularly important in Greek cuisine, being used to flavor everything from soups and sauces to cakes and pastries. Apricots, cherries, dates, figs, grapes, melons, peaches, plums and pomegranates are among the many fruits which flourish, but there are also some more "old fashioned" fruits such as quinces and medlars which are also very popular.

Apricots, dates, figs and peaches are among those which are dried, and all sorts of fruits are also preserved in syrup and served to guests in a small dish accompanied by a glass of water.

The most important fruit grown in Greece is the olive, and the olive tree and its fruit has always been central to the daily lives of the Greeks. Not only the fruit and oil are used but the beautiful grained wood is made into furniture. Nuts are widely used in Greek cooking, particularly almonds, pine nuts, pistachio nuts and walnuts.

PASTA, RICE & BREAD

Although pasta does not have the significance it has in Italy, it is very popular in Greece, and spaghetti, macaroni and orzo, particularly, often appear on the menu.

The Greeks learned breadmaking from the Egyptians and, as in all Mediterranean countries, it is still extremely important. A wide variety of loaves and rolls can be seen in any baker's shop, from flat pita bread to elaborately braided loaves. There are several traditional breads which are made for special festivals.

Rice is grown in Greece and is an important item in the Greek diet. It is used in both sweet and savory dishes.

SWEET DISHES

Although many of the Greek pastries, cakes and desserts are extremely sweet, often dripping with syrup or honey, the overall sugar consumption is half that in the United States. Such sweet dishes are reserved for special occasions.

EATING PATTERNS

A typical day's eating pattern begins early with a breakfast consisting of bread and olive oil with feta cheese and olives. On cold mornings in more mountainous regions, farm workers eat a large hot breakfast before going out to work on the land.

Nowadays, people living in the cities and working in offices generally have bread or toast with marmalade and butter, but they may also have tomatoes, olives, cheese or salami.

Lunch may be eaten any time between noon and 3 p.m. It may be simply a dish of beans and grains, sometimes accompanied with salted herrings or sardines. Fried eggs with fried potatoes or French fries is a popular lunch!

A salad is always served with lunch. In the summer it consists of lettuce with tomatoes and cucumber, often with olives, raw onion and feta cheese. In winter the salads are usually made with finely shredded cabbage dressed with olive oil and lemon or vinegar.

A glass of wine may be drunk with lunch. It is usually followed by a 'siesta'! Lunch may be more substantial and could start with meze or soup. There is no general rule and habits change according to the season.

The evening meal may start with soup which is usually followed by fried fish or a meat dish and cooked vegetables or salad. Desserts are rarely eaten after an everyday meal as they tend to be associated with Sundays and feast days. Fruit is eaten but not necessarily after a meal; it may be a mid-afternoon snack accompanied by a small cup of black coffee.

STREET LIFE

The sociable temperament of the Greeks and the warm climate encourages street life and there are numerous cafés, milk bars and street stalls serving delicious snacks such as yogurts, ice creams, pastries and roast chestnuts. Pastry shops serve cakes and sweet pastries with drinks such as fruit nectars, lemonade or black coffee.

DRINKS

At home alcohol is rarely drunk on its own, but as an accompaniment to food and it is generally only served when entertaining. Sweet fruit drinks and mineral water are normally served with a meal. Greek hospitality is such that it is impossible to visit a Greek home without being offered something to drink, and a drink is never served without something to eat. Coffee might be accompanied by preserved fruits in syrup and other drinks will be served with anything from a few olives to a complete array of mezes.

POPULAR INGREDIENTS

Cheese: Feta cheese is a white, salty cheese stored in strong brine. It is traditionally made from unpasteurised ewes' milk but the imported feta cheese is generally made from cows' milk. It is most frequently used in salads but can also be used in cooked pastries. Cottage cheese can sometimes be used as a substitute. Kefalotiri is a strong cheese which is good for grating. Parmesan or a well-flavored Cheddar may be used instead. Haloumi is a soft- to semi-soft goats' milk cheese which is quite salty and yet mild. It is generally served toasted or fried.

Tomatoes: Greek tomatoes are sweet and full of flavor. At times when our own tomatoes do not have much flavor it is preferable to use canned tomatoes. Even when using fresh tomatoes it may be necessary to add a little sugar to bring out the flavor.

Rigani: The dried leaves and flowers of a Mediterranean marjoram. It is sold in Greek delicatessens but is not widely available, so oregano has been used instead in the recipes here because it is closer to rigani than marjoram.

Olives: Greek olives come in all shapes, colors and sizes. The best known ones outside Greece are the sweet-sour Kalamata olives.

Olive oil: Many Greek recipes are given their distinctive flavor by the use of good quality olive oil. Where possible extra-virgin olive oil should be used as it has the strongest flavor, but sometimes a less-pronounced flavor is required and then refined olive oil or sunflower oil may be used.

Pine nuts: These are not really nuts but are kernels from cones of a pine tree. They are expensive, but have a very distinctive resinous flavor and there is really no substitute for them.

Orzo: A rice-shaped pasta which may be difficult to find outside specialist shops. Any other small or "soup" pasta may be used, or even rice.

Honey: The finest Greek honey is the fragrant Hymettus honey, and no other flower honeys, such as lavender or orange blossom should be substituted for it. If the recipe does not specify a fragrant honey a blended honey will give satisfactory results.

Yogurt: Where yogurt is used in recipes in this book, thick Greek yogurt – which is now widely available – should be used. Sheeps' or cows' milk yogurt may be used, although sheeps' milk yogurt is richer and creamier.

Filo pastry: Filo pastry is known as Phyllo in Greece. There are various pastry brands available and they are not a standard size. The pastry dough used in the recipes in this book comes in long narrow packages containing 20-24 sheets, measuring approximately 12 x 20 in. When handling filo pastry, it is important to keep the sheets in a pile covered with a damp cloth and work with one sheet at a time, layering it or filling it, otherwise the pastry dough will dry out.

Orange-flower water: Many of the sweet dishes in this book contain orange-flower water, which gives a fragrant flavor to fruit dishes.

Rosewater: Like orange-flower water, rosewater is used in many sweet dishes, particularly milk-based desserts. It should be labeled as "triple distilled". If it is bought from a drugstore it may be mixed with glycerin.

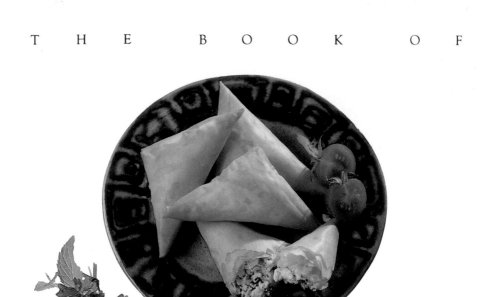

—CHEESE & HERB TRIANGLES—

1/4 pound feta cheese
1/2 cup cottage cheese
1/2 beaten egg
1 tablespoon chopped fresh parsley
1 tablespoon chopped fresh mint
1 tablespoon snipped fresh chives
Pepper
4 sheets filo pastry
1/4 cup butter

Into a bowl, crumble feta cheese. Add cottage cheese, egg, parsley, mint, chives and pepper. Blend together with a fork.

Preheat oven to 375F (190C). Butter a baking sheet. Lay the sheets of dough in a pile on a work surface. Keep covered while working with one sheet at a time. In a small saucepan melt butter. Brush one sheet of dough with butter. Cut it into 4 long strips.

Place a teaspoon of filling in one corner of dough strip. Fold a corner of dough over filling. Turn triangle over and over to the end of the strip. Repeat with remaining dough. Brush tops of triangles with butter. Bake in the oven 10 to 12 minutes or until crisp and brown.

Makes 16.

──MARINATED FETA CHEESE──

3/4 pound feta cheese
2 garlic cloves
1/2 teaspoon mixed peppercorns
8 coriander seeds
1 bay leaf
Fresh oregano and thyme sprigs
Olive oil, to cover
Bread, toasted, cut into squares, to serve

With a sharp knife, cut feta cheese into cubes. Cut garlic into thick slivers.

With a mortar and pestle, lightly crush peppercorns and coriander seeds.

Into a jar with a tight-fitting lid, pack cubes of cheese with the bay leaf, interspersing layers of cheese with garlic, peppercorns, coriander and oregano or thyme. Pour in enough olive oil to cover cheese. Cover and refrigerate 2 weeks. Serve on hot toast, sprinkled with a little of the oil from the jar.

Makes 6 servings.

HERB & FETA BALLS

1 cup cream cheese (8 ounces), softened
3/4 cup crumbled feta cheese (3 ounces)
1 garlic clove, crushed
1 teaspoon chopped fresh parsley
1 teaspoon chopped fresh mint
2 tablespoons sesame seeds, 1 tablespoon finely
    chopped fresh parsley and 1 tablespoon finely
    chopped fresh mint, to garnish
Grape leaves, to serve
Kumquat or yellow tomato wedges, to garnish

In a small bowl, mix together cream cheese and feta cheese until smooth. Stir in garlic, parsley and mint.

Roll cheese into 20 balls. Chill at least 1 hour. Meanwhile, toast sesame seeds for garnish: put in a skillet and heat until seeds are golden-brown, stirring frequently. Let cool.

To garnish, mix together chopped parsley and chopped mint. Roll half of the cheese balls in herbs and half in toasted sesame seeds. Serve on grape leaves and garnish with kumquat or yellow tomato wedges.

Makes 20.

SPANAKOPITTA

1 pound frozen spinach
2 tablespoons extra-virgin olive oil
1 small onion, finely chopped
1 garlic clove, crushed
2 tablespoons chopped fresh cilantro
1/2 teaspoon freshly grated nutmeg
1 cup crumbled feta cheese (4 ounces)
1 egg, lightly beaten
Salt and pepper
1/4 cup butter
4 sheets filo pastry
Cilantro leaves, to garnish

Cook spinach according to package directions. Drain and chop.

Preheat oven to 350F (175C). Butter an 8-inch square pan. In a skillet, heat oil, then add onion and garlic and cook until onion is soft. Add drained spinach; cook, stirring, 2 more minutes. Let cool slightly. Stir in cilantro, nutmeg and cheese. Add beaten egg and mix well. Season. In a small pan, melt butter. Brush one sheet of dough with butter. Lay it in pan, pressing well down into corners. Let excess dough hang over edges of pan.

Brush a second sheet of dough with butter and lay it in pan at right angles to first sheet. Repeat with remaining dough. Spoon spinach mixture into pan. Fold excess dough over filling to cover. Leave dough in slight folds. Brush with melted butter. Bake in oven 40 minutes or until golden-brown and crisp. Cut into 9 squares. Serve hot, warm or cold, garnished with cilantro leaves.

Makes 9 servings.

– GRAPE LEAF-WRAPPED CHEESE –

8 vacuum-packed small grape leaves
8 ounces haloumi cheese
2 teaspoons chopped fresh cilantro
Salt and pepper
2 teaspoons extra-virgin olive oil
TO SERVE:
8 thick slices, long thin Greek bread
1 garlic clove

The remaining grape leaves may be frozen for use another time.

Rinse grape leaves thoroughly in several changes of cold water. Pat dry. Cut cheese into 8 cubes. Toss cheese in chopped cilantro, then season with salt and pepper. Wrap each piece of cheese in a grape leaf. Brush with oil. Preheat broiler and broil cheese packages a few minutes, turning once or twice until cheese heats through.

Toast bread on both sides. Cut the garlic clove in half and rub the toasted bread with the cut surfaces. Serve the toast with the broiled cheese packages.

Makes 8 servings.

IMAM BAYALDI

2 small eggplants
Salt
1/4 cup extra-virgin olive oil
1 large onion, chopped
1 garlic clove, crushed
1 red bell pepper, seeded and chopped
2 tablespoons tomato paste
2 ounces sun-dried tomatoes in oil, drained and
  chopped
1/2 teaspoon sugar
1 teaspoon wine vinegar
Pepper
Toasted pine nuts and cilantro leaves, to garnish

Cut eggplants into 1/4-inch slices. Sprinkle with salt and put into a colander to drain 30 minutes. Preheat oven to 350F (175C). In a skillet, heat 2 tablespoons of the olive oil, add onion, garlic and bell pepper. Cook about 10 minutes until onion is soft. Add tomato paste, sun-dried tomatoes, sugar, vinegar and pepper.

Pat eggplant slices dry with paper towels. Arrange slices in a baking pan. Put a tea-spoonful of tomato mixture onto each egg-plant slice. Drizzle remaining olive oil over and around eggplants. Cover pan and bake 40 to 50 minutes until eggplants are tender. Serve garnished with toasted pine nuts and cilantro leaves.

Makes 6 servings.

EGGPLANT SALAD

2 eggplants
1 garlic clove, crushed
2 tablespoons mayonnaise
2 tablespoons plain yogurt
Salt and pepper
2 tablespoons chopped fresh parsley
Pita bread and raw vegetables, to serve

Bring a saucepan of water to a boil. Add eggplants to pan and cook about 30 minutes or until quite soft.

Drain eggplants. As soon as they are cool enough to handle, with a teaspoon, cut them down the middle and scrape the flesh away from the skins. Let cool. Put eggplant flesh, garlic, mayonnaise and yogurt in a food processor and process until smooth. Season to taste with salt and pepper.

Transfer eggplant puree to a serving bowl. Cover and refrigerate 1 hour. Garnish with parsley and serve with pita bread and raw vegetables.

Makes 6 servings.

ZUCCHINI SALAD

2 tablespoons pine nuts
1 pound zucchini
2 tablespoons extra-virgin olive oil
1 garlic clove, crushed
2 tablespoons dried currants
2 teaspoons chopped fresh mint
Juice of 1/2 lemon
Salt and pepper
2 green onions

In a large skillet, cook pine nuts, stirring, until just beginning to brown. Remove pine nuts and reserve. Trim zucchini and slice thinly.

In a medium-size skillet, heat oil and add zucchini, garlic, currants and pine nuts. Cook, stirring, until zucchini are just beginning to soften and brown slightly.

Stir in mint, lemon juice, salt and pepper. Transfer to a serving dish and leave until cold. Slice the green onions and scatter them over the top.

Makes 8 servings.

──FRIED HALOUMI SALAD──

A selection of salad greens, such as Lollo Rosso, Mache
  lettuce, arugula and purslane
1/2 pound haloumi cheese
1 egg, beaten
1 cup fresh bread crumbs
Vegetable oil for deep-frying
Marigold petals, to garnish
SALAD DRESSING:
1/3 cup olive oil
1 tablespoon balsamic vinegar
1 teaspoon fresh lemon juice
1 teaspoon Dijon-style mustard
Salt and pepper

Rinse and dry salad greens. Arrange on 6
individual plates.

To make dressing, in a jar with a tight-fitting
lid, shake together oil, vinegar, lemon juice,
mustard, salt and pepper. Cut cheese into
1/2-inch cubes. Put beaten egg in a shallow
bowl and bread crumbs on a board or plate.
Toss cheese in egg, then in bread crumbs to
coat.

Heat oil in a deep-fryer. Fry cheese until
golden-brown. Drain on paper towels. Pour
the dressing over the salad. Arrange cheese
cubes on each plate. Sprinkle with marigold
petals and serve immediately.

Makes 6 servings.

TOMATO SALAD

1/2 pound small tomatoes
1/2 small red onion
10 to 12 ripe olives
Greek bread, to serve
DRESSING:
1/4 cup extra-virgin olive oil
1 tablespoon fresh lemon juice
1 teaspoon chopped fresh mint
2 teaspoons snipped fresh chives
1 teaspoon honey
Salt and pepper

To make dressing, in a small bowl, mix together olive oil, lemon juice, mint, chives, honey, salt and pepper.

With a sharp knife, cut tomatoes into slices. Slice onion thinly. Place in a serving bowl with olives.

Stir dressing and pour over tomatoes, onions and olives. Toss together to coat tomatoes with dressing. Serve with Greek bread.

Makes 4 servings.

Variation: Add cubes of feta cheese.

GARLIC-PEPPER SALAD

1 small green bell pepper
1 small red bell pepper
1 small yellow bell pepper
1 small purple bell pepper
2 garlic cloves, finely chopped
1/2 cup extra-virgin olive oil
1 tablespoon fresh lemon juice
1 tablespoon balsamic vinegar
Salt and pepper
Chopped fresh parsley, basil leaves and nasturtium
　flowers (optional), to garnish

With a sharp knife, cut all the bell peppers into quarters. Remove seeds and cores.

Preheat broiler. Broil peppers, skin side up, until black and blistered. Put in a plastic bag and leave 10 minutes, then scrape off the blistered skins. Slice peppers lengthwise in strips.

Arrange on a serving dish in groups of alternating colored strips. Sprinkle with chopped garlic. In a small bowl, beat together oil, lemon juice, vinegar, salt and pepper, then pour mixture over the peppers. Let marinate 2 to 3 hours. Serve garnished with chopped parsley, basil leaves and nasturtium flowers, if available.

Makes 6 servings.

MARINATED OLIVES

1/4 pound green olives
2 thin lemon slices
2 teaspoons coriander seeds
2 garlic cloves
Extra-virgin olive oil, to cover
1/4 pound ripe olives
1/4 red bell pepper
1 small hot chile pepper
1 fresh thyme sprig

Place green olives in a jar with a tight-fitting lid. Cut each lemon slice into quarters and add to olives. Lightly crush coriander seeds and 1 of the garlic cloves and add to the green olives. Cover with olive oil and seal jar.

Place ripe olives in a separate jar. Crush remaining garlic and cut pepper and chile into strips, removing seeds. Add to olives with thyme. Cover with olive oil and seal jar.

Refrigerate 2 days before transferring to a serving bowl and serving with other appetizers. If the jars are resealed the olives will keep indefinitely. The oil can be used for salad dressings and cooking.

Makes 6 servings.

BEAN DIP

2 tablespoons extra-virgin olive oil
1 onion, finely chopped
1-1/3 cups (1/2 pound) dried lima beans, soaked
    overnight, then drained
Juice of 1/2 lemon
1 teaspoon sugar
Salt and pepper
1 teaspoon paprika
1 tablespoon chopped fresh dill
2 red bell peppers
Paprika, olive oil and fresh dill sprigs, to garnish
Pita bread and raw vegetables, to serve

In a large saucepan, heat 1 tablespoon of the oil over medium heat. Add onion and cook until soft, stirring occasionally. Add 2 cups water and beans. Bring to a boil, and boil 10 minutes, then reduce heat and simmer, covered, 1-1/2 hours or until very soft. Add more water if necessary. Drain beans, reserving the water. In a food processor, process beans, remaining oil, lemon juice, sugar, salt, pepper, paprika and chopped dill, adding enough cooking water to make a smooth puree. Cover closely with plastic wrap and cool. If not serving immediately, refrigerate.

Cut bell peppers in half and scoop out seeds. Stand pepper halves on a flat plate and fill with bean puree. Garnish with a sprinkle of paprika, a drizzle of olive oil and a dill sprig. Serve with pita bread and sticks of raw vegetables.

Makes 8 servings.

TZATZIKI

1 cucumber
2-1/2 teaspoons salt
1 garlic clove
1 tablespoon chopped fresh mint
1 cup plain yogurt, sheep's milk preferred
Pepper
Mint leaves, to garnish
Pita bread, to serve

With a sharp knife, peel cucumber and cut into small dice. Place in a colander, sprinkle with 2 teaspoons salt and let drain 1 hour.

Pat cucumber dry with paper towels. Crush garlic with remaining salt until creamy.

In a bowl, mix together garlic, chopped mint and yogurt. Season with pepper. Stir in diced cucumber. Transfer to a serving bowl. Garnish with mint leaves and serve at once with pita bread.

Makes 6 servings.

STUFFED TOMATOES

1/2 cup long-grain rice
4 large or 8 medium-size tomatoes
4 green onions, chopped
2 garlic cloves, crushed
2 teaspoons chopped fresh mint
Salt and pepper
4 teaspoons olive oil
Toasted pine nuts, to garnish (optional)

In a saucepan of boiling salted water, cook rice 7 to 8 minutes, or until just tender. Drain and rinse well.

Preheat oven to 350F (175C). Cut a thin slice off the top of each tomato. Carefully scoop out the flesh and place it in a strainer to drain. Chop half the flesh (the remainder can be saved for sauces or soup). Put chopped flesh in a bowl with rice, green onions, garlic, mint, salt and pepper.

Place tomatoes in a baking dish and fill them with stuffing. Drizzle a little olive oil over each tomato. Cover dish and bake 25 to 30 minutes (less for smaller tomatoes) or until soft but still holding their shapes. Garnish with toasted pine nuts, if desired.

Makes 4 servings.

——CORIANDER MUSHROOMS——

1/2 pound small button mushrooms
1 teaspoon coriander seeds
3 tablespoons extra-virgin olive oil
1 teaspoon fresh lemon juice
9 tablespoons dry white wine
1 garlic clove, crushed
1 fresh thyme sprig
Salt and pepper
4 tablespoons chopped fresh parsley, to garnish

Wipe mushrooms with a damp cloth and trim stems. Crush coriander seeds in a mortar and pestle.

In a medium-size skillet, heat oil. Add coriander seeds and heat them a few seconds. Add lemon juice, white wine, garlic, thyme, salt and pepper and bring to a boil. Add mushrooms to pan, stir well, cover and simmer 10 minutes.

With a slotted spoon, transfer mushrooms to a serving dish. Boil liquid 1 to 2 minutes to reduce a little, then pour it over the mushrooms. Let cool completely. Sprinkle chopped parsley over the top before serving.

Makes 8 servings.

——— BROILED VEGETABLES ———

1 red bell pepper
2 baby zucchini
2 baby eggplants
1 fennel bulb
8 baby corn-on-the-cob
Salt and pepper
Zucchini flowers and basil sprigs, to garnish
MARINADE:
2/3 cup extra-virgin olive oil
2 garlic cloves, crushed
1 teaspoon chopped fresh parsley
1 teaspoon chopped fresh mint
1 teaspoon chopped fresh oregano

To make marinade, in a bowl, mix together olive oil, garlic, parsley, mint and oregano. Cut bell pepper lengthwise into quarters. Remove seeds and core. Cut zucchini in half lengthwise. Cut eggplants in half lengthwise. Cut fennel bulb into quarters. Put pepper, zucchini, eggplants, fennel and corn into the bowl with the marinade. Leave at least 1 hour.

Preheat broiler or grill. Broil vegetables about 10 minutes, or until tender. Turn them every few minutes and brush with marinade. Season with salt and pepper. Garnish with zucchini flowers and basil sprigs.

Makes 8 servings.

Variation: A wide variety of vegetables can be prepared this way. Try mushrooms, tomatoes, Belgium endive, onions and squashes.

LEEKS A LA GRECQUE

8-10 young small leeks
3 tablespoons extra-virgin olive oil
2 tablespoons fresh lemon juice
1 garlic clove, crushed
Salt and pepper
1 tablespoon chopped fresh mint
Slivers of sun-dried tomatoes and mint leaves, to
  garnish

With a sharp knife, cut root ends off leeks and trim tops down to white parts. Wash very carefully.

In a non-reactive saucepan, put olive oil, lemon juice, 1/2 cup water, garlic, salt and pepper. Bring to a boil. Add leeks, cover and cook 10 to 15 minutes or until leeks are tender.

Transfer leeks to a serving dish. If there is a lot of liquid, boil to reduce and thicken slightly, then pour it over the leeks. Scatter chopped mint over the top and leave until cool. Serve garnished with slivers of sun-dried tomatoes and mint leaves.

Makes 8 servings.

Variation: Substitute pearl onions for leeks.

FRIED EGGPLANT

2 small eggplants
Salt
Vegetable oil for frying
2 lemons, cut into quarters
BATTER:
1 cup all-purpose flour
Pinch of salt
2 tablespoons butter, melted
3/4 cup lukewarm water
1 egg white

To make batter, into a large bowl, sift flour and salt. Add melted butter and water, beating to form a smooth, creamy batter. Let stand 1 hour.

Slice eggplants into 1/4-inch slices. Place in a colander, sprinkle with salt and let drain 30 minutes. In a bowl, whisk egg white until stiff but not dry. Fold into batter. Pat eggplant slices dry with paper towels.

In a skillet, heat 1/2 inch oil. Dip eggplant slices into batter. Fry in batches 2 minutes, then turn over and fry a further 2 minutes until crisp and golden on both sides. Drain on paper towels. Keep warm while frying remaining slices. Serve at once, with lemon quarters.

Makes 6 servings.

——STUFFED ZUCCHINI RINGS——

1/2 cup bulgur wheat
6 zucchini, each about 6 inches long
1 tablespoon extra-virgin olive oil
1 small onion, finely chopped
2 teaspoons tomato paste
1 teaspoon chopped fresh mint
Salt and pepper
2 tablespoons fresh lemon juice
Fresh grape leaves, to serve
Fresh herbs, to garnish

Put bulgur wheat into a bowl. Pour in enough boiling water to come well above the wheat. Let soak 1 hour. Drain thoroughly.

Preheat oven to 350F (175C). Cut rounded ends off zucchini. With a small apple corer, carefully remove centers from zucchini. In a small skillet, heat oil. Add onion and cook until soft. Remove from heat. Stir in bulgur wheat, tomato paste, mint, salt and pepper. Press stuffing firmly into hollowed-out zucchini.

Place zucchini in a baking dish. Pour lemon juice and 1/4 cup water over zucchini. Cover dish and bake 45 minutes, or until zucchini are .tender but still firm enough to slice neatly. With a sharp knife, cut zucchini into 1/8-inch slices. Serve on a plate lined with grape leaves. Garnish with fresh herbs.

Makes 6 servings.

DOLMADES

20 vacuum-packed grape leaves
1 cup boiling water
1/2 cup long-grain rice
3 tablespoons extra-virgin olive oil
1 small onion, finely chopped
1/3 cup pine nuts
1/4 cup raisins
2 tablespoons chopped fresh mint
1/4 teaspoon ground cinnamon
Salt and pepper
2 tablespoons tomato paste
2 teaspoons fresh lemon juice
Lemon slices and fresh mint, to garnish (optional)

Rinse grape leaves and place in a saucepan of boiling water. Simmer 5 minutes. Drain. In a small saucepan, combine the 1 cup boiling water and rice, cover and simmer until rice is almost cooked. Drain, if necessary. In a skillet, heat 2 tablespoons of the oil. Add onion and cook until soft. Add pine nuts and cook until lightly browned. Stir in raisins, mint, cinnamon, salt, pepper and rice. Let cool.

Trim stems from grape leaves. Place a little filling on each leaf. Fold sides over and roll up. Line a saucepan with any damaged leaves. Place dolmades side by side in pan, to fit tightly. In a bowl, mix 1-1/4 cups water, the remaining olive oil, tomato paste and lemon juice. Pour over dolmades. Place a plate on top. Cover pan and simmer 1 to 1-1/2 hours or until liquid is absorbed and leaves are tender. Garnish with lemon and mint, if desired, and serve hot.

Makes 20.

TARAMASALATA

1/4 pound smoked cod's roe
3 slices white bread, crusts removed
2 garlic cloves, crushed
Juice of 1 lemon
1/3 cup extra-virgin olive oil
1/4 cup plain yogurt
1/2 teaspoon paprika
1/2 small onion, grated
30 to 40 cherry tomatoes and slivered ripe olives, to
   serve

With a sharp knife, scrape cod's roe from skin and put into a blender or food processor fitted with the metal blade.

Soak bread in a little water, then crumble into blender or processor. Process until smooth. With the motor running, add garlic, lemon juice, olive oil, yogurt and paprika. Add more lemon juice or olive oil if necessary for flavor or consistency. Finally add onion. Process until smooth.

Cut tops off tomatoes and carefully scoop out flesh and seeds. Leave upside down on paper towels 30 minutes. Spoon taramasalata into tomatoes. Top each one with a sliver of ripe olive.

Makes 6 servings.

FRIED SQUID

1-1/2 pounds small squid
All-purpose flour seasoned with salt and pepper
Vegetable oil for deep-frying
BATTER:
1 cup all-purpose flour
Pinch of salt
2 tablespoons butter, melted
3/4 cup lukewarm water
1 egg white
GREEN MAYONNAISE:
1 bunch watercress, washed and trimmed
1 tablespoon boiling water
1-1/4 cups mayonnaise

To make batter, into a large bowl, sift flour and salt. Add melted butter, then gradually add lukewarm water, beating continuously to form a smooth, creamy batter. Let stand 1 hour. To make mayonnaise, in a food processor, puree watercress with boiling water. In a bowl, mix watercress puree and mayonnaise. Set aside.

Clean squid. Pull on tentacles; cut off just above heads, discarding heads and viscera. Pull out the transparent sword-shape pen. Rinse body, pulling away outer skin. Pat dry with paper towels. Cut body and tentacles into rings. In a bowl, whisk egg white until stiff but not dry. Fold into batter. Heat oil in a deep-fryer. Dip squid into seasoned flour, then into batter. Fry a few pieces at a time or until brown and crisp. Drain. Serve with mayonnaise.

Makes 6 servings.

SEAFOOD PARCELS

2/3 cup butter
1/4 cup all-purpose flour
2/3 cup milk
2 tablespoons fresh lemon juice
1 garlic clove, crushed
1 tablespoon each chopped fresh mint, chopped fresh
    cilantro and chopped fresh parsley
Pinch of red (cayenne) pepper
Pinch of paprika
1/2 teaspoon ground cumin
Salt
3 ounces cooked mussels
2 ounces cooked shelled shrimp
2 ounces cooked squid or white fish
6 sheets filo pastry, thawed if frozen

Preheat oven to 375F (190C). In a saucepan, melt 2 tablespoons of the butter. Stir in flour, then gradually stir in milk. Stirring, cook sauce until thick. Stir in lemon juice, garlic, mint, cilantro, parsley, cayenne, paprika, cumin and salt. Remove from heat. Gently stir in mussels, shrimp and squid or white fish.

Melt remaining butter. Brush over 1 sheet filo dough, place another sheet on top and butter it. Repeat with 2 more sheets of dough. Cut into 12 squares. Butter remaining 2 sheets of dough. Place one on top of the other. Cut in half. Pile the 4 sheets together; cut into 6 squares. Place some filling in middle of each square. Draw dough up and pinch together to form pouches. Place on a baking sheet. Bake 30 minutes or until brown and crisp.

Makes 18.

BROILED MUSSELS

20 mussels
1/2 onion, chopped
1 bouquet garni
1 garlic clove, finely chopped
1 tablespoon chopped fresh fennel
1 tablespoon chopped fresh oregano
Salt and pepper
1/2 cup fresh bread crumbs
1/2 cup extra-virgin olive oil
Fresh fennel sprigs, to garnish

Scrub mussels and remove beards. Discard any which do not close when tapped. Put into a saucepan with 1-1/4 cups water, onion and bouquet garni.

Cover, bring to a boil and cook 1 to 2 minutes, shaking pan occasionally, or until mussels have opened; discarding those that remain closed. Strain. Remove top half of each shell. In a bowl, mix together garlic, fennel, oregano, salt, pepper and bread crumbs.

Preheat broiler. Arrange mussels in a flame-proof serving dish. Sprinkle with bread crumb mixture. Pour about 1 teaspoon of olive oil over each mussel. Place mussels under broiler until heated through and browned. Serve garnished with fennel sprigs.

Makes 8 servings.

──────── SWORDFISH KABOBS ────────

Juice of 1/2 lemon
1/4 cup extra-virgin olive oil
1 tablespoon chopped fresh fennel
1 tablespoon chopped fresh chives
1 garlic clove, crushed
Salt and pepper
1 pound swordfish
1 small onion
16 cherry tomatoes
Lemon slices and sea beans, to garnish

In a bowl, mix together lemon juice, olive oil, fennel, chives, garlic, salt and pepper. Cut swordfish into 3/4-inch cubes. Place in bowl of marinade and let stand 1 hour. Cut onion into quarters and separate layers.

Preheat broiler. Thread swordfish, onion and tomatoes onto 8 skewers. Broil 5 to 10 minutes, turning frequently and brushing with any remaining marinade. Serve garnished with lemon slices and sea beans.

Makes 8 servings.

MEATBALLS IN TOMATO SAUCE

1 slice bread, crusts removed
1 pound ground lamb
1 garlic clove, crushed
1 onion, finely chopped
1 tablespoon chopped fresh parsley
1 tablespoon chopped fresh mint
1/2 teaspoon ground cinnamon
Salt and pepper
2 tablespoons extra-virgin olive oil
Fresh herbs, to garnish
TOMATO SAUCE:
1 tablespoon extra-virgin olive oil
1 small onion, chopped
1 (14-oz.) can chopped tomatoes
1 teaspoon sugar

Soften bread in a little water. Squeeze dry, then crumble into a medium-size bowl. Add lamb, garlic, onion, parsley, mint, cinnamon, salt and pepper to bowl and mix thoroughly. On a floured board, roll meat mixture into small balls.

To make the sauce, in a saucepan, heat oil. Add onion and cook until soft. Add tomatoes, salt, pepper and sugar. Cook gently 5 minutes. In a blender or food processor, process sauce until smooth. Return to pan and reheat. In a skillet, heat oil and fry meatballs 5 to 6 minutes or until browned and cooked through, turning frequently. Transfer to a warmed serving dish and pour sauce over the top. Garnish and serve.

Makes 6 servings.

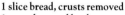

——GROUND MEAT PASTRIES——

1 tablespoon pine nuts
1/4 cup extra-virgin olive oil
1 onion, finely chopped
1 pound lean ground beef
1 teaspoon ground cinnamon
1 tablespoon chopped fresh parsley
Salt and pepper
6 sheets filo pastry, thawed if frozen
1 recipe Tzatziki, see page 25, to serve

In a skillet, fry pine nuts in a little oil until golden. Remove from pan and set aside.

In the same skillet, heat 2 tablespoons of the oil. Add onion and cook until soft. Stir in beef and cook, stirring, a few minutes or until brown all over. Add cinnamon, parsley, pine nuts, salt and pepper. Cook 10 minutes, then let cool.

Preheat oven to 350F (175C). Cut each sheet of dough into 3 long strips. Brush strips with remaining oil. Spread 1 teaspoon of filling in a line on one end of each strip, leaving a small margin on each side. Roll over twice and fold long sides over the edge, then continue rolling to make a tube. Place on a baking sheet. Bake 20 to 30 minutes or until crisp and golden. Serve with Tzatziki.

Makes 18.

KEFTEDES

2 slices white bread, crusts removed
3/4 pound lean ground beef
1 tablespoon chopped fresh dill
1/2 teaspoon ground cumin
1 small egg, beaten
1 teaspoon ouzo
Salt and pepper
Flour for dusting
3 tablespoons extra-virgin olive oil
Fennel sprigs and lemon wedges, to garnish
SAUCE:
2/3 cup plain yogurt
1 tablespoon chopped fresh cilantro

Soak bread in a little water. Squeeze dry and crumble into a bowl.

Add ground beef, dill, cumin, egg, ouzo, salt and pepper. Mix thoroughly. Spread meat mixture onto a plate. Divide into 16 equal-size portions. Roll each into a ball, then flatten to form a patty. Put some flour on a plate; dip each patty into flour.

To make the sauce, in a bowl, mix together yogurt and cilantro and season with salt and pepper. In a skillet, heat oil. Fry keftedes 3 to 4 minutes on each side until well browned and cooked through. Garnish with fennel sprigs and lemon wedges and serve with the yogurt sauce.

Makes 16.

PORK KABOBS

1 pound lean pork
1 onion
1 green bell pepper
8 cherry tomatoes
MARINADE:
Juice of 1/2 orange
2 tablespoons extra-virgin olive oil
1 garlic clove, crushed
1 teaspoon chopped fresh thyme
1 teaspoon coriander seeds, crushed
Salt and pepper
Shredded lettuce, orange slices and fresh thyme sprigs,
    to garnish

To make the marinade, in a bowl, mix together orange juice, oil, garlic, thyme, coriander seeds, salt and pepper. Cut pork into 3/4-inch cubes and add to marinade. Mix thoroughly, cover and refrigerate 2 hours. Cut onion into quarters and separate the layers. Cut bell pepper into small squares, removing core and seeds.

Thread pork, onion, pepper and tomatoes onto 8 bamboo skewers. Preheat grill or broiler. Cook, turning occasionally, 10 to 15 minutes or until pork is cooked through. Serve on a bed of shredded lettuce, garnished with orange slices and fresh thyme.

Makes 8.

SOUVLAKIA

2 garlic cloves, crushed
1/4 cup fresh lemon juice
2 tablespoons extra-virgin olive oil
4 tablespoons chopped fresh oregano
Salt and pepper
1 pound lean lamb
6 bay leaves
Fresh oregano sprigs, to garnish
RED PEPPER SAUCE:
1 tablespoon extra-virgin olive oil
1 small onion, chopped
2 red bell peppers, chopped
1 cup chicken stock

In a bowl, mix together garlic, lemon juice, olive oil, oregano, salt and pepper. Cut lamb into 3/4-inch cubes. Add lamb to marinade and stir to coat lamb with marinade. Cover and refrigerate 2 hours. To make the sauce, in a saucepan, heat oil, add onion and cook until soft. Add bell peppers and cook 5 minutes. Pour in stock and simmer 10 minutes. Press through a strainer or puree in a blender or food processor.

Thread lamb onto skewers, placing bay leaves on skewers at intervals. Preheat grill or broiler. Cook, turning occasionally, 10 minutes or until lamb is brown and crisp on the outside and pink and juicy inside. Garnish with oregano and serve with the sauce.

Makes 6 servings.

—CUCUMBER & YOGURT SOUP—

1 large cucumber
2-1/2 cups plain yogurt
2 teaspoons fresh lemon juice
2 tablespoons chopped fresh mint
Salt and pepper
1-1/4 cups chilled milk
Snipped fresh chives, to garnish

Rinse cucumber and trim ends; do not peel. Into a bowl, grate cucumber quite finely.

Stir in yogurt, lemon juice and mint. Season well with salt and pepper. Cover bowl and refrigerate 2 hours.

Stir in milk. Pour soup into 6 individual bowls. Sprinkle snipped chives over soup and serve.

Makes 6 servings.

AVGOLEMONO SOUP

4-1/2 cups well-flavored chicken stock
Salt and pepper
2 tablespoons long-grain rice
2 eggs
1/4 cup fresh lemon juice
6 lemon slices and tarragon sprigs, to garnish

In a saucepan, heat chicken stock. Season with salt and pepper. Bring to a boil. Add rice to chicken stock. Cover pan and simmer 10 to 15 minutes or until rice is cooked.

In a bowl, beat together eggs and lemon juice. Strain into another bowl. Add a ladleful of hot stock to egg mixture. Whisk and pour back into pan.

Heat gently, stirring, 3 to 4 minutes or until soup thickens. Do not boil. Pour into 6 warmed soup bowls. Serve garnished with a lemon slice and tarragon sprigs.

Makes 6 servings.

Note: The best chicken stock for this recipe is made from the liquid saved from boiling a chicken.

FISHERMAN'S SOUP

1 (2-1/2-lb.) fish, such as snapper or sea bass, ready to
  cook
2 onions, sliced
1/3 cup extra-virgin olive oil
2 bay leaves
2 fresh parsley sprigs
1 small fresh thyme sprig
4 tomatoes, peeled and coarsely chopped
8 peppercorns
Salt
8 jumbo shrimp, preferably raw
16 mussels, cleaned, (see page 36)
2 to 3 teaspoons fresh lemon juice
Chopped fresh parsley, to garnish
Croutons made from French loaf

Skin and fillet fish. In a large saucepan, put
fish bones, onions, olive oil, bay leaves,
parsley, thyme, tomatoes, peppercorns and
salt. Add 1-1/4 quarts water and bring to a
boil. Reduce heat and simmer, uncovered, 45
minutes. Press through a strainer into a
clean pan.

Cut fish into 1-inch cubes. Bring stock to a
simmer. Add fish and shrimp, if raw. Simmer
5 minutes, or until fish is nearly cooked. Do
not overcook, or it will disintegrate. Finally,
add mussels and cooked shrimp, if using.
Cook 1 to 2 minutes or until mussels open.
Add lemon juice to taste. Garnish the soup
with parsley and serve with the croutons.

Makes 8 servings.

BEAN SOUP

1 pound dried haricot beans
1 leek
1 onion
2 carrots
3 celery stalks with leaves
1/4 cup extra-virgin olive oil
2 garlic cloves, crushed
2 tablespoons tomato paste
Salt and pepper
Chopped fresh parsley and chopped ripe olives, to
   garnish

Into a bowl, put beans. Add enough boiling water to cover. Let stand 1 hour.

Drain the beans and rinse, then put in a large saucepan. Add 2-3/4 quarts water, bring to a boil and boil 10 minutes. Reduce heat and simmer 30 minutes. Meanwhile, slice leek, onion, carrots and celery. In a saucepan, heat oil. Add leek, onion, carrots, celery and garlic. Stir to coat vegetables with oil, then cover pan and cook gently 5 minutes.

When beans have cooked 30 minutes, add vegetables and tomato paste, then cover and cook 1 to 1-1/2 hours or until beans are tender and beginning to split. Season with salt and pepper. Add more water if needed. Serve garnished with chopped parsley and olives.

Makes 6 to 8 servings.

—— LENTIL & TOMATO SOUP ——

2 tablespoons extra-virgin olive oil
1 large onion, chopped
2 garlic cloves, chopped
3 celery stalks, chopped
1 (14-oz.) can chopped tomatoes
1-1/4 cups brown lentils
2 tablespoons chopped fresh parsley
1 bay leaf
Salt and pepper
1 tablespoon fresh lemon juice
Yogurt and 1 tablespoon each chopped fresh basil and
    mint, to garnish

In a large saucepan, heat oil. Add onion and garlic and cook until soft. Add celery, tomatoes, lentils, parsley and bay leaf to pan. Stir in 2-1/4 quarts water and bring to a boil. Cover pan and simmer 1-3/4 hours or until soup is thick and lentils and vegetables are very soft.

In a blender or food processor fitted with the metal blade, puree soup until smooth. Return to saucepan. Soup should be thick, but add more water if a thinner consistency is preferred. Season well. Add lemon juice. Serve soup in warmed bowls with a spoonful of yogurt floating in center and herbs scattered over the top.

Makes 6 to 8 servings.

Note: This soup may be served without being pureed, if preferred.

-CUCUMBER & TOMATO SALAD-

4 tomatoes
1/2 cucumber
1 bunch green onions
1 bunch purslane or watercress, well rinsed
1/3 cup extra-virgin olive oil
2 tablespoons fresh lemon juice
1 teaspoon chopped fresh mint
1 teaspoon chopped fresh fennel
Salt and pepper
Halved stuffed olives, to garnish

Put tomatoes into a bowl. Pour boiling water over tomatoes and let stand 1 minute, then put into cold water. Leave 1 minute, peel, cut into small dice and put into a bowl.

With a sharp knife, peel cucumber, cut into small dice and add to tomatoes. Trim and chop green onions and add to tomato and cucumber.

Break the purslane or watercress into small sprigs. Mix with tomato and cucumber. In a bowl, whisk together olive oil, lemon juice, mint, fennel, salt and pepper. Pour over salad. Serve garnished with halved stuffed olives.

Makes 4 servings.

SQUID SALAD

1 pound small squid
1/4 cup extra-virgin olive oil
1 small red onion, finely chopped
2 tablespoons dry white wine
1 garlic clove, crushed
Salt and pepper
1 tablespoon fresh lemon juice
1 tablespoon chopped fresh parsley
Lemon zest strips and parsley sprigs, to garnish

To clean squid, pull on tentacles and cut them off just above head, discarding head and viscera. Pull out sword-shaped transparent pen.

Rinse body inside and out, pulling away pink outer membrane. Dry on paper towels. Cut body into 1/4-inch rings and cut tentacles into small pieces. In a skillet, heat 2 tablespoons of the oil. Add onion and cook until soft and just beginning to color. Add squid and fry gently 5 minutes, stirring. Add wine and garlic. Cook, covered, 5 to 10 minutes, until squid is tender.

Let cool in pan. Transfer squid and onion to a serving dish. Add remaining oil, salt, pepper, lemon juice and parsley to pan. Stir, then spoon it over the squid. Serve garnished with lemon zest and parsley sprigs.

Makes 4 servings.

THREE BEAN SALAD

3 ounces dried flageolet beans
3 ounces dried red kidney beans
2 fresh thyme sprigs
1 pound fresh fava beans, shelled
1 small onion, finely chopped
Red bell pepper rings, to garnish
DRESSING:
1/2 cup extra-virgin olive oil
Juice of 1 lemon
1 tablespoon chopped fresh mint
1 tablespoon chopped fresh parsley
Salt and pepper

Put flageolet and kidney beans in 2 separate bowls.

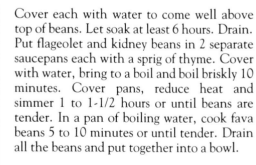

Cover each with water to come well above top of beans. Let soak at least 6 hours. Drain. Put flageolet and kidney beans in 2 separate saucepans each with a sprig of thyme. Cover with water, bring to a boil and boil briskly 10 minutes. Cover pans, reduce heat and simmer 1 to 1-1/2 hours or until beans are tender. In a pan of boiling water, cook fava beans 5 to 10 minutes or until tender. Drain all the beans and put together into a bowl.

To make the dressing, in a bowl, mix together oil, lemon juice, mint, parsley, salt and pepper. Pour dressing over warm beans. Add chopped onion and mix well. Cover and refrigerate until chilled, then transfer to a serving dish. Serve garnished with bell pepper rings.

Makes 6 servings.

COUNTRY SALAD

2 heads leaf lettuce
6 tomatoes
1/2 cucumber
1 bunch green onions
2 tablespoons chopped fresh mint
2 teaspoons chopped fresh oregano
1/4 cup extra-virgin olive oil
2 tablespoons fresh lemon juice
Salt and pepper
6 ounces feta cheese
12 ripe olives

Wash and dry lettuce. Roll up the leaves and slice across to make shreds. Arrange them on a serving dish.

Cut tomatoes into quarters and arrange on lettuce. Score down side of cucumber with a fork or knife to make grooves, then slice cucumber and arrange on lettuce. Chop green onions and sprinkle them over the salad with mint and oregano.

In a bowl, mix together oil, lemon juice, salt and pepper. Pour over salad. Cut feta cheese into cubes and arrange on the salad with olives. Serve immediately.

Makes 6 servings.

———— SNOW PEA SALAD ————

1 pound fresh snow peas
1/4 cup extra-virgin olive oil
Juice of 1/2 lemon
Salt and pepper
1 garlic clove
1 tablespoon chopped fresh cilantro
1 tablespoon chopped fresh mint
Lemon zest strips, to garnish

Remove ends and any strings from snow peas.
In a large saucepan, heat 1 tablespoon of the
oil, add snow peas and stir to coat with oil.

Add enough water to cover snow peas. Bring
to a boil, cover and cook about 5 minutes or
until snow peas are crisp-tender. Drain and
return to pan.

Pour lemon juice and remaining oil over
snow peas. Add salt and pepper and mix well.
Turn into a serving dish and let cool. Before
serving, chop garlic finely and scatter over
snow peas with cilantro and mint; garnish
with lemon zest.

Makes 4 to 6 servings.

LENTIL SALAD

1-1/4 cups green lentils
1/4 cup extra-virgin olive oil
1 onion, finely chopped
3 tomatoes, peeled and chopped
Salt and pepper
1 tablespoon chopped fresh parsley
2 tablespoons fresh lemon juice
Onion rings, chopped fresh parsley and lemon slices, to
    garnish

Put lentils into a bowl, cover with cold water
and let soak 3 to 4 hours. Drain well.

In a large saucepan, heat oil, add onion and
cook until soft. Add tomatoes and cook 1
minute, then add lentils. Cover with water,
cover pan and simmer 30 minutes, adding
water if necessary, or until lentils are tender,
yet still hold their shapes and all water has
been absorbed.

Add salt, pepper, parsley, lemon juice and
remaining oil to lentils. Mix carefully, then
transfer to a serving dish and let cool. Serve
garnished with onion rings, chopped parsley
and lemon slices.

Makes 4 to 6 servings.

— GREEN BEANS WITH ONION —

1 pound green beans
3 tablespoons extra-virgin olive oil
2 medium-size onions, chopped
1 garlic clove, crushed
4 teaspoons tomato paste
3/4 cup water
1 tablespoon chopped fresh oregano
Salt and pepper
Finely chopped red bell pepper or oregano sprig, to
    garnish

Trim ends from beans. In a large saucepan, heat oil. Add onions and garlic and cook 5 to 10 minutes or until soft.

Add beans to onion. Mix tomato paste with water. Pour tomato mixture over beans, then add more water, if necessary, to just cover beans.

Add oregano, salt and pepper. Cover pan and simmer 15 to 20 minutes or until beans are tender. Remove lid and boil to reduce the liquid. Serve garnished with chopped bell pepper or oregano sprig.

Makes 4 servings.

—FAVA BEANS & ARTICHOKES—

1-1/2 pounds fresh fava beans, shelled
1 (14-oz.) can artichoke hearts
1 tablespoon extra-virgin olive oil
1 teaspoon cornstarch
1 tablespoon fresh lemon juice
1 tablespoon chopped fresh parsley
Salt and pepper
Chopped fresh parsley, to garnish

In a saucepan of boiling water, cook fava beans 10 minutes or until tender. Drain, reserving 1/4 cup of the water.

Drain and rinse artichoke hearts, then cut in half. In a saucepan, heat olive oil. Add fava beans and artichokes. In a small bowl, mix cornstarch and lemon juice and stir into reserved cooking water. Stir parsley, salt and pepper into cornstarch mixture.

Pour cornstarch mixture over beans and artichokes. Bring to a boil and cook until sauce is slightly thickened. Serve with more parsley sprinkled over the top.

Makes 6 servings.

──── FAVA BEANS WITH DILL ────

2 pounds fresh fava beans
1/4 cup extra-virgin olive oil
1 onion, finely chopped
1 garlic clove, crushed
2 tablespoons chopped fresh dill
Salt and pepper
Dill sprigs, to garnish
Yogurt, to serve

Shell fava beans. In a saucepan, heat oil. Add onion and garlic and cook over low heat until just beginning to color.

Add fava beans and cook 2 to 3 minutes. Add enough hot water to just cover beans, stir in chopped dill and season with salt and pepper. Cook, covered, 10 minutes, or until beans are tender.

When beans are tender, remove lid and cook briskly until liquid has almost evaporated. Garnish with dill sprigs and serve with yogurt.

Makes 6 servings.

BEANS & GREENS

1-1/3 cups dried beans (8 ounces)
1 garlic clove
Bouquet garni of fresh thyme, parsley and oregano
1 pound Swiss chard or young cabbage leaves, shredded
Salt and pepper
2 tablespoons extra-virgin olive oil
1 tablespoon fresh lemon juice
Lemon slices, to garnish

Put beans into a bowl, cover with cold water and let soak about 6 hours. Drain well.

Into a saucepan, put beans. Add enough cold water to come 2 inches above beans. Add garlic and bouquet garni. Bring to a boil and boil briskly 10 minutes. Cover pan, reduce heat and simmer 1 to 1-1/2 hours or until beans are tender.

Add shredded Swiss chard or cabbage and simmer gently 5 minutes or until chard is tender. Drain thoroughly. Return to pan, and stir in salt, pepper, olive oil and lemon juice. Serve garnished with lemon slices.

Makes 4 to 6 servings

Note: This dish may also be served cold, if preferred.

—BLACK-EYED PEAS & RICE—

1-1/3 cups dried black-eyed peas (8 ounces)
1 tablespoon fresh lemon juice
2 tablespoons extra-virgin olive oil
1 large onion, finely chopped
1 garlic clove, crushed
1/2 cup long-grain rice
Salt and pepper
2 tablespoons white-wine vinegar
Chopped fresh herbs and green olives, to garnish

Rinse and drain peas and place in a saucepan. Cover with cold water and bring to a boil and boil 2 minutes.

Drain peas, discarding water. Return peas to pan, cover with fresh water to come well above surface of peas. Add lemon juice. Bring to a boil. Cover, reduce heat and simmer 20 to 30 minutes or until peas are tender.

In another saucepan, heat oil and add onion and garlic and cook until soft. Add rice, stir to coat with oil, then add 3/4 cup water and season with salt. Bring to a boil, cover pan and simmer 10 to 15 minutes or until rice is tender and water absorbed. Drain peas and mix with rice. Add vinegar, salt and pepper. Heat together 2 minutes. Serve garnished with chopped herbs and olives.

Makes 4 to 6 servings.

FASOULIA

1/4 cup extra-virgin olive oil
1 garlic clove, crushed
3 large tomatoes, peeled and chopped
1-1/3 cups dried haricot beans (8 ounces), soaked
   overnight
1 bay leaf
1 fresh thyme sprig
Salt and pepper
Onion rings and fresh thyme sprigs, to garnish

In a large saucepan, heat oil. Add garlic and tomatoes, and cook a few minutes or until tomatoes soften.

Drain beans and add to pan. Pour in boiling water to come 1 inch above top of beans. Add bay leaf and thyme. Cover pan and simmer 1 to 1-1/4 hours or until beans are tender.

The liquid should have reduced to form a thick sauce. If not, simmer uncovered a few minutes. Discard bay leaf and thyme. Season with salt and pepper. Transfer beans to a serving dish. Serve garnished with onion rings and thyme sprigs.

Makes 4 servings.

POURGOURI PILAF

1 onion
2 tomatoes
1 small green bell pepper
2 tablespoons extra-virgin olive oil
1 ounce vermicelli
1-1/3 cups bulgur wheat
1-1/2 cups chicken stock
Salt and pepper
Fresh cilantro sprigs, to garnish

With a sharp knife, slice onion thinly. Put tomatoes in a bowl; pour boiling water over and leave 1 minute.

Transfer tomatoes to a bowl of cold water. Leave another minute. Drain and peel off skins. Cut tomatoes in half, then slice. Quarter bell pepper and remove core and seeds, then slice. In a large saucepan, heat oil, add onion and pepper and cook until onion is soft. Add vermicelli and stir to coat with oil.

Put bulgur wheat in a colander and rinse with cold water, then add to pan. Stir in chicken stock and bring to a boil. Cover pan and simmer 5 minutes. Add tomatoes and simmer 5 to 10 minutes or until bulgur wheat is tender and stock is absorbed. Add more water if necessary. Stir in salt and pepper. Transfer to a serving dish and garnish with cilantro.

Makes 6 servings.

POTATO KEPHTEDES

1 pound potatoes
2 tomatoes, peeled
1 tablespoon extra-virgin olive oil
Salt and pepper
1 tablespoon chopped fresh parsley
4 green onions, finely chopped
1/2 cup all-purpose flour, sifted
Vegetable oil for frying
Rings of green part of green onions and fresh dill sprigs,
    to garnish

Peel potatoes and cut into equal-size pieces.

Put potatoes into a pan of water, bring to a boil and cook, covered, 20 minutes or until tender. Drain and let cool. Cut tomatoes into quarters, remove seeds and chop flesh. Add tomatoes, olive oil, salt, pepper, parsley, green onions and flour to potatoes. Mix thoroughly.

Knead mixture lightly. On a floured board, roll out to a thickness of 1/2 inch. Cut out 8 circles. In a skillet, heat oil. Fry potato cakes 6 to 7 minutes, turning once or until golden and crisp. Serve at once, garnished with green onions and dill.

Makes 8 servings.

─────SPINACH & RICE─────

1 pound fresh spinach
1 bunch green onions
1/4 cup extra-virgin olive oil
1 tablespoon chopped fresh dill
3/4 cup long-grain rice
1-1/4 cups hot water
Salt and pepper
Fresh dill sprigs and chopped tomato, to garnish

Trim stems from spinach and rinse leaves well. In a saucepan, put spinach and just the water that clings to leaves. Cook 5 minutes.

Drain spinach thoroughly and let cool, then squeeze dry and chop. Cut green onions (including some of green part) into thin slices. In a saucepan, heat oil, add green onions and cook until soft. Add spinach and dill. Simmer 5 minutes.

Put rice in a strainer and rinse under running water. Drain and then add to spinach. Stir rice until coated with oil. Add hot water. Bring to a boil, then cover pan, reduce heat and simmer 15 to 20 minutes or until rice is cooked and water is absorbed. Add salt and pepper. Press rice into 6 ramekins or cups. Turn out onto warmed plates. Serve garnished with dill and chopped tomato.

Makes 6 servings.

─── ZUCCHINI WITH CHEESE ───

1-1/2 pounds zucchini
2 tablespoons extra-virgin olive oil
1 large onion, chopped
1 teaspoon chopped fresh mint
2 eggs
1-1/2 cups grated kefalotiri cheese (6 ounces)
1/4 teaspoon grated nutmeg
Salt and pepper

Preheat oven to 350F (175C). Trim zucchini ends, then cut into 1/2-inch slices. Put zucchini slices into a steamer above boiling water and steam a few minutes or until crisp-tender. Cook in batches, if necessary.

In a skillet, heat oil, add onion and cook until soft. Mix zucchini and mint with onion, then put in a baking dish.

In a bowl, beat eggs with cheese, nutmeg, salt and pepper, then pour over the zucchini. Bake 20 minutes, or until top is lightly browned.

Makes 4 servings.

Variation: This dish may also be made with summer squash.

——————OKRA & TOMATOES——————

1 pound small okra
1/4 cup olive oil
1 small onion, chopped
1 small leek, chopped
1 pound tomatoes, peeled and chopped
1 garlic clove, crushed
1 tablespoon fresh lemon juice
Salt and pepper
1 teaspoon sugar
Chopped fresh parsley, to garnish

With a sharp knife, cut stems off okra. Rinse pods, drain well and pat dry. Do not pierce pods.

In a large shallow pan, heat oil. Add onion and leek and cook slowly until soft and lightly colored. Add okra and turn carefully in the oil. Cook 5 minutes.

Add tomatoes, garlic, lemon juice, salt, pepper and sugar. Cover pan and simmer 10 minutes. Remove lid and cook 10 minutes or until okra is tender and sauce reduced to a small quantity. If sauce reduces too quickly, add a little water. Garnish with chopped parsley and serve.

Makes 6 servings.

FISH PLAKI

2 tablespoons extra-virgin olive oil
2 onions, sliced
2 garlic cloves, crushed
4 large tomatoes, peeled and chopped
Juice of 1/2 lemon
2 tablespoons chopped fresh parsley
1 bay leaf
1 teaspoon dried oregano
Salt and pepper
2 pounds bream
Chopped green olives, to garnish

In a saucepan, heat oil. Add onions and garlic and cook gently 5 to 10 minutes or until soft.

Stir in tomatoes, lemon juice, parsley, bay leaf, oregano, salt and pepper. Cover and simmer 10 minutes. Meanwhile, preheat oven to 400F (205C).

Place fish in a baking dish and top with tomato mixture. Bake 20 to 30 minutes or until fish is just beginning to flake when tested with a fork. Sprinkle chopped olives over fish and serve at once.

Makes 4 servings.

— FRIED FISH WITH SKORDALIA —

2 pounds fish fillets, such as cod
Flour seasoned with salt and pepper
Vegetable oil for deep-frying
BATTER:
1 cup all-purpose flour
1 teaspoon chopped fresh parsley
2 tablespoons butter, melted
3/4 cup lukewarm water
1 egg white
SKORDALIA:
3 garlic cloves, crushed
2-inch thick slice white bread
1-1/4 cups ground blanched almonds
1/2 cup extra-virgin olive oil
2 teaspoons fresh lemon juice

To make the batter, into a large bowl, sift flour and a pinch of salt. Stir in parsley. Add melted butter and gradually add water, beating to form a smooth, creamy batter. Let stand 1 hour. Meanwhile, make the Skordalia. Put garlic in a blender or food processor fitted with the metal blade. Remove crust from bread. Squeeze bread in a little cold water, then add to garlic with ground almonds and a little olive oil.

With the motor running, gradually add remaining oil. Stir in lemon juice and salt and pepper to taste. In a bowl, whisk egg white, then fold into batter mixture. Heat oil in a deep-fryer. Cut fish into 6 pieces. Dip in seasoned flour, then in batter. Fry 8 to 10 minutes, according to thickness of fish. Drain on paper towels, then serve with the Skordalia.

Makes 6 servings.

— SHRIMP & SAFFRON SAUCE —

Juice of 1/2 lemon
3 tablespoons extra-virgin olive oil
2 garlic cloves, crushed
1 tablespoon chopped fresh fennel
Salt and pepper
16 raw jumbo shrimp
Lemon slices and fennel sprigs, to garnish
SAFFRON SAUCE:
2/3 cup fish stock
4 saffron threads
2/3 cup mayonnaise
1 teaspoon fresh lemon juice

In a bowl, mix together lemon juice, oil, garlic, fennel, salt and pepper.

Put shrimp into a dish and pour the marinade over them. Cover and refrigerate 2 hours. To make the saffron sauce, in a saucepan, boil fish stock until reduced to 1 tablespoon. Add saffron threads. Let cool. Strain stock into a bowl and stir in the mayonnaise. Add lemon juice, salt and pepper.

Preheat broiler. Thread shrimp onto skewers and broil 10 minutes, turning once. Remove from skewers. Garnish with lemon slices and fennel and serve with Saffron Sauce.

Makes 4 servings.

—— SHRIMP & FETA TARTS ——

6 ounces shelled cooked shrimp
4 ounces feta cheese
Fresh basil leaves, to garnish
PASTRY:
1-1/2 cups all-purpose flour
1/2 teaspoon salt
3 tablespoons extra-virgin olive oil
1 egg, beaten
TOMATO SAUCE:
2 tablespoons extra-virgin olive oil
1 onion, chopped
1 garlic clove, crushed
Half (14-oz.) can chopped tomatoes
1 tablespoon chopped sun-dried tomato
2 teaspoons chopped fresh basil
Salt and pepper

To make Pastry, into a bowl, sift flour and salt. With a fork, mix in olive oil, egg and 1 to 2 teaspoons water to make a firm dough. Knead lightly, wrap in plastic wrap and refrigerate 1 hour. To make Tomato Sauce, in a skillet, heat oil. Add onion and garlic and cook until soft. Add tomatoes. Cook 5 to 10 minutes or until sauce is very thick. Stir in basil, salt and pepper. Preheat oven to 400F (205C).

On a floured surface, roll out dough thinly. Line 4 (4-inch) loose-bottom tart pans with dough and press a piece of foil into each. Bake 10 minutes. Remove foil; bake 5 minutes. Divide shrimp among pastry cases. Crumble cheese over shrimp. Spread Tomato Sauce over cheese and shrimp. Bake 5 minutes. Serve garnished with basil leaves.

Makes 4 servings.

──── SQUID & SHRIMP KABOBS ────

3/4 pound cleaned squid, see page 34
Juice of 1/2 lemon
2 teaspoons honey
2 tablespoons extra-virgin olive oil
8 large raw shelled shrimp
Salt and pepper
Lemon slices and chopped fresh parsley, to garnish
GARLIC MAYONNAISE:
4 garlic cloves
1-1/2 cups prepared mayonnaise
Lemon juice to taste

With a sharp knife, cut squid into 1/4-inch rings. In a bowl, mix together lemon juice, honey and oil. Add squid. Cover and refrigerate 6 hours. To make the mayonnaise, crush garlic to a smooth pulp using a mortar and pestle. Put garlic and mayonnaise into a blender or food processor. Process to combine. Stir in lemon juice to taste.

Preheat broiler. Drain squid and pat dry with paper towels. Thread onto soaked wooden skewers, alternating with shrimp. Season with salt and pepper. Broil 4 to 5 minutes, turning constantly or until golden. Cut lemon slices in half and dip cut edges in chopped parsley. Garnish kabobs with the lemon slices and serve with the mayonnaise.

Makes 4 servings as an appetizer.

─── BROILED SARDINES ───

2 pounds fresh sardines, cleaned and scaled
2 tablespoons coarse sea salt
1 tablespoon chopped fresh oregano
1 tablespoon chopped fresh parsley
1 tablespoon chopped fresh fennel
Lemon slices, to garnish
AVGOLEMO SAUCE:
1-3/4 cups fish stock
Salt and pepper
1 tablespoon cornstarch
2 large egg yolks
Juice of 1 lemon

Slash each sardine twice on each side. Sprinkle with sea salt and put herbs inside cavities. Let stand 30 minutes. To make the sauce, in a saucepan, put fish stock. Season and bring to a boil. In a bowl, mix cornstarch with a little water. Whisk hot stock into cornstarch mixture. Return to pan. Simmer 10 to 15 minutes, stirring, or until sauce thickens. In a bowl, beat egg yolks. Stir in lemon juice. Add a little of hot sauce; return sauce to pan. Simmer, stirring, until thickened. Do not boil.

Preheat broiler. Broil sardines 1-1/2 to 2 minutes on each side, until skins are brown and crisp. Garnish with lemon slices and serve with sauce.

Makes 4 servings.

——— SQUID WITH RED WINE ———

1-1/2 pounds squid
1/4 cup extra-virgin olive oil
1 large onion, chopped
2 garlic cloves, crushed
1 pound tomatoes, peeled and coarsely chopped
2/3 cup red wine
Salt and pepper
1/2 teaspoon sugar
1-inch cinnamon stick
1 tablespoon chopped fresh parsley
6 bread slices, crusts removed, and 3 tablespoons olive oil, to serve

Clean squid, see page 34. Cut into rings. Dry thoroughly with paper towels. In a large saucepan, heat oil. Add onion and garlic and cook until soft. Add squid and fry until lightly browned. Add tomatoes, wine, salt, pepper, sugar and cinnamon. Simmer, uncovered, 30 minutes, or until squid is tender. Stir in parsley.

Sauce should be thick and rich. If not, transfer squid to a hot dish and boil sauce to reduce. Cut bread into triangles. In a skillet, heat oil and fry bread until golden on both sides. Serve squid in individual dishes, with fried bread tucked around the sides.

Makes 6 servings.

BAKED GRAY MULLET

2 tablespoons extra-virgin olive oil
2 red onions, thinly sliced
1 garlic clove, crushed
1 fresh fennel sprig
1 fresh parsley sprig
2 pounds gray mullet, cleaned
Salt and pepper
1/2 cup dry white wine
1 cup bread crumbs
Fennel sprigs, to garnish

Preheat oven to 350F (175C). In a skillet, heat oil. Add onions and cook gently 10 minutes or until soft.

Put garlic, fennel and parsley in the cavity of the fish. Season fish with salt and pepper, inside and out.

Spread softened onions over bottom of a baking dish. Place fish on onions and add wine. Sprinkle with bread crumbs. Cover dish and bake 10 minutes, then uncover dish and cook 10 to 15 minutes or until fish just begins to flake when tested with a knife. Garnish with fennel sprigs.

Makes 4 servings.

Variation: 4 small mullet could be used instead of 1 large one.

STUFFED EGGPLANT

3 eggplants
Salt and pepper
Extra-virgin olive oil
1 onion, finely chopped
1 pound ground lamb or beef
2 tomatoes, peeled and chopped
1 tablespoon tomato paste
1 tablespoon chopped fresh oregano
1/2 teaspoon ground cinnamon
1/4 cup dry white wine
CHEESE SAUCE:
2 tablespoons butter
3/4 cup all-purpose flour
1-1/4 cups milk
3/4 cup grated kefalotiri cheese (3 ounces)

Cut eggplants lengthwise, from stem, sprinkle with salt and let drain 1 hour. In a saucepan, heat oil. Add onion and cook until soft. Add lamb and stir until brown. Add tomatoes, tomato paste, oregano, cinnamon, salt, pepper, wine and 1/4 cup water. Cover and simmer 15 minutes, stirring occasionally. Remove lid and cook until mixture is dry, stirring frequently. Pat eggplants dry with paper towels. Scoop out pulp. Chop half and mix with meat mixture (reserve other half for another dish).

Preheat oven to 350F (175C). To make the sauce, in a saucepan, melt butter. Stir in flour and cook 2 minutes, stirring, over low heat. Remove from heat. Gradually stir in milk. Return to heat. Stir until thick and smooth. Simmer 5 minutes, stirring. Season with salt and pepper. Stir in two-thirds of cheese. Fill each eggplant shell two-thirds full of meat mixture. Place in a casserole dish. Top with sauce. Sprinkle with remaining cheese. Bake 20 minutes or until cheese is lightly browned.

Makes 6 servings.

MOUSSAKA

1-1/2 pounds eggplant
Salt and pepper
1 tablespoon extra-virgin olive oil plus extra for frying
2 onions, finely chopped
1-1/2 pounds ground lamb or beef
2 tomatoes, peeled and chopped
2 tablespoons tomato paste
1 tablespoon chopped fresh oregano
1 teaspoon ground cinnamon
1/2 cup dry white wine
WHITE SAUCE:
1/4 cup butter
1/2 cup all-purpose flour
2 cups milk
2/3 cup plain yogurt
1/4 cup grated kefalotiti cheese (1 ounce)

Thinly slice eggplant and put into a colander. Sprinkle with salt and let drain 1 hour. In a saucepan, heat 1 tablespoon oil. Add onions and cook until soft. Add lamb and stir until brown. Add tomatoes, tomato paste, oregano, cinnamon, salt, pepper, wine and 1/2 cup water. Cover; simmer 30 minutes. Remove lid and cook until mixture is dry. Pat eggplants dry with paper towels. Heat 1/2 inch oil in a skillet. Fry eggplants, turning once, until beginning to brown. Drain on paper towels. Preheat oven to 350F (175C).

To make sauce, melt butter. Stir in flour and cook 2 minutes over low heat. Remove from heat. Gradually stir in milk and yogurt. Return to heat. Stir until thick and smooth. Simmer 5 minutes. Season with salt and pepper. Put a layer of eggplant in a baking dish. Cover with half of meat mixture, then half of remaining eggplant slices. Cover with remaining meat and eggplant slices. Pour sauce over top. Sprinkle with cheese. Bake 40 minutes or until brown.

Makes 6 servings.

——LAMB STEAKS WITH PASTA——

4 thick lamb leg steaks
Salt and pepper
2 garlic cloves, sliced
2/3 cup water
1 (14-oz.) can chopped tomatoes
1/3 cup extra-virgin olive oil
1 tablespoon chopped fresh marjoram
1 tablespoon chopped fresh parsley
1-1/4 cups boiling water
10 ounces orzo (rice-shaped pasta)
Salad leaves, to serve

Preheat oven to 400F (205C). Season meat with salt and pepper. Place in a large roasting pan.

Scatter garlic over meat. Add the 2/3 cup water, tomatoes, olive oil, marjoram and parsley. Cook 40 minutes, basting occasionally and turning lamb over.

Add 1-1/4 cups boiling water and the pasta. Stir in more salt and pepper. Cook about 40 minutes or until pasta is cooked. If necessary, add more hot water. Serve with salad greens.

Makes 6 servings.

LAMB PASTRIES

12 grape leaves, preserved in brine
1/4 cup extra-virgin olive oil
Juice of 1/2 lemon
2 garlic cloves, crushed
1 tablespoon chopped fresh marjoram
Salt and pepper
6 thin lamb steaks or pieces of lamb fillet
6 sheets filo pastry
1/4 cup butter, melted
Shredded nasturtium flowers and mint, to garnish

Soak grape leaves in water 1 hour. In a sauce-pan of boiling water, cook grape leaves 5 minutes. Drain and dry on paper towels.

In a bowl, mix together olive oil, lemon juice, garlic, marjoram, salt and pepper. In a dish, place lamb, pour marinade over and let marinate in a cool place 1 hour.

Preheat oven to 375F (190C). Brush each sheet of dough with butter. Lay a grape leaf in middle of one end of each sheet. Place a lamb steak on top, then cover with another grape leaf. Fold sides of dough over lamb and roll up to form neat packages. Place on a baking sheet. Bake 20 to 30 minutes or until pastry is golden and crisp. Serve garnished with shredded nasturtium flowers and mint.

Makes 6 servings.

BAKED LAMB WITH VEGETABLES

1 leg of lamb, about 4-1/2 pounds
3 garlic cloves, cut into slivers
Salt and pepper
1 eggplant, sliced
1-1/2 pounds potatoes, peeled
1 large onion, thinly sliced
1 pound tomatoes, sliced
1/4 cup white wine
1 tablespoon chopped fresh oregano

Preheat oven to 425F (220C). Cut slits in meat and insert slivers of garlic. Rub generously with salt and pepper. Place lamb in a large roasting pan and put in oven.

Reduce heat to 350F (175C) and roast 1-1/2 hours for slightly pink meat or 2 hours for medium-well done. Meanwhile, slice eggplant into 1/4-inch slices, place in a colander and sprinkle with salt. Let drain 30 minutes, then rinse and pat dry.

One hour before the end of cooking time, remove any fat from roasting pan and add vegetables. Add wine, season with salt and pepper and sprinkle with oregano. Return to the oven. Turn vegetables over during cooking to cook them evenly in juices. Carve lamb into slices, adding any meat juices to vegetables. Serve lamb with the vegetables and meat juices.

Makes 6 servings.

—— SPICED RACK OF LAMB ——

1 tablespoon all-purpose flour
Salt and pepper
2 racks of lamb
1 garlic clove, finely chopped
2 tablespoons extra-virgin olive oil
1 pound tomatoes, coarsely chopped
1/2 lemon, chopped
1 cinnamon stick
3 whole cloves
1 small red chile, seeded and chopped
1/2 cup dry white wine
2 tablespoons tomato paste
Lemon slices, to garnish

Preheat oven to 350F (175C). Mix together flour, salt and pepper. Rub over lamb. Press garlic into gaps between bones. In a roasting pan, heat oil. Put lamb, skin-side down, in oil to brown. Remove lamb. Add tomatoes, lemon, cinnamon, cloves and chile to roasting pan. Return lamb, skin-side up, to pan.

In a bowl, mix together wine, 1/2 cup water and tomato paste. Pour over lamb. Cover pan loosely with foil. Roast 1 hour. Remove foil and roast 30 minutes or until lamb is cooked to desired doneness. Cut lamb into individual chops and keep warm. Place roasting pan on heat and boil liquid to reduce to a thick sauce. Pour over meat. Garnish with lemon.

Makes 6 servings.

——————— PORK WITH PEARS ———————

2 tablespoons extra-virgin olive oil
2 onions, chopped
2 pounds boned lean pork, cut into cubes
1 cup red wine
Grated zest of 1/2 orange
1/2 cinnamon stick
Salt and pepper
1-1/4 cups water
2 pears
2 teaspoons honey
Chopped fresh cilantro leaves, orange peel strips and
   pita bread, to garnish

In a flameproof casserole dish, heat oil. Add
onions and cook until soft. Push to side of
pan, turn up heat and brown meat in batches.

Add wine, orange zest, cinnamon stick, salt,
pepper and water. Bring to a simmer, then
cover casserole and cook 1 hour.

Peel, core and slice pears and place on top of
meat. Drizzle honey over pears. Cover pan
and simmer 30 to 40 minutes or until meat is
tender. Garnish with chopped cilantro
leaves, strips of orange peel and pita bread.

Makes 6 servings.

Note: This recipe is traditionally made with
quinces. If quinces are available, use them
instead of pears.

AFELIA

1-1/4 pounds pork tenderloin
1 teaspoon coriander seeds
1 teaspoon brown sugar
Salt and pepper
1 tablespoon extra-virgin olive oil
1 cup red wine
Fresh cilantro leaves, to garnish

With a sharp knife, cut pork into 1/2-inch slices. Place slices between 2 sheets of waxed paper and beat with a mallet or rolling pin to flatten slightly.

With a mortar and pestle, lightly crush coriander seeds with sugar and salt and pepper to taste. Sprinkle crushed mixture onto both sides of pork. Let stand in a cool place at least 30 minutes.

In a skillet, heat oil. Add pork in batches and brown on both sides. Return pork to skillet, pour in the wine, boil 1 minute, then reduce heat and cook, uncovered, 20 to 30 minutes or until pork is tender. The liquid should have reduced to a syrupy consistency. If not, transfer pork to a serving dish and keep hot. Boil liquid until reduced, then pour it over the meat and garnish with cilantro leaves.

Makes 4 servings.

———— SPICY BRAISED BEEF ————

1 (3-lb.) beef round roast
2 garlic cloves, crushed
1/2 teaspoon ground cinnamon
1/4 teaspoon ground cloves
Salt and pepper
3 tablespoons extra-virgin olive oil
4 onions, thinly sliced
1/2 cup red wine
2 tablespoons tomato paste
1 pound spaghetti
1 tablespoon balsamic vinegar
Fresh herbs, to garnish

With a sharp knife, make slits in the beef.

In a bowl, mix garlic, cinnamon, cloves, salt and pepper. Press mixture into slits and let beef stand in a cool place 1 hour. In a flame-proof casserole dish into which meat will just fit, heat oil. Turn meat in hot oil until brown all over. Remove from casserole dish. Add onions and cook gently until soft and lightly browned. Replace meat. Add the wine and enough hot water to barely cover it. Mix tomato paste with a little water; stir into casserole. Season with salt and pepper.

Cover pan and simmer about 1-1/2 hours, turning meat frequently, or until it is tender. Bring a large pan of salted water to a boil and cook spaghetti until al dente. Remove meat and keep hot. Add vinegar to sauce. Boil briskly until reduced to a smooth glossy sauce. Slice beef. Garnish with herbs and serve with some sauce poured over beef and remainder stirred into spaghetti.

Makes 6 servings.

PASTITSIO

2 tablespoons extra-virgin olive oil
1 onion, chopped
1 garlic clove, crushed
1 pound ground beef
1-1/4 cups beef stock
2 teaspoons tomato paste
1/2 teaspoon ground cinnamon
1 teaspoon chopped fresh mint
Salt and pepper
1/2 pound macaroni
1/4 cup butter
1/2 cup all-purpose flour
2 cups milk
1/2 cup plain yogurt
1-1/2 cups grated kefalotiri cheese (6 ounces)

Preheat oven to 375F (190C). In a skillet, heat oil. Add onion and garlic and cook until soft. Add beef and stir until browned. Stir in stock, tomato paste, cinnamon, mint, salt and pepper. Simmer 10 to 15 minutes or until sauce is reduced. Meanwhile, in a pan of boiling water, cook macaroni 8 minutes or until tender. Drain, rinse with cold water and set aside.

In a saucepan, melt butter. Stir in flour and cook 1 minute. Gradually stir in milk and yogurt and simmer 5 minutes. Stir in half the cheese. Season with salt and pepper. Mix macaroni into cheese sauce. Spread half the macaroni mixture over bottom of a large gratin or souffle dish. Cover with meat sauce, then top with remaining macaroni. Sprinkle remaining cheese over top. Bake 45 minutes or until browned.

Makes 4 to 6 servings.

SOFRITO

1/4 cup extra-virgin olive oil
1 onion, finely chopped
1 garlic clove, crushed
1-1/2 pounds thin veal slices
All-purpose flour seasoned with salt and pepper
2 tablespoons brandy
2/3 cup white wine
1-1/4 cups beef stock
Salt and pepper
3 tablespoons chopped fresh parsley
Extra parsley, to garnish

In a skillet, heat oil. Add onion and garlic, and cook until soft. Transfer to a flameproof casserole dish.

Coat meat lightly with seasoned flour. Fry in skillet until brown on both sides. Add brandy. When brandy has stopped bubbling, transfer meat to casserole.

Add wine, stock, salt and pepper to casserole dish. Cover and simmer 45 minutes or until meat is tender and sauce is lightly thickened. Stir in parsley. Garnish with more parsley.

Makes 6 servings.

- VEAL CHOPS WITH TOMATOES -

2 tablespoons extra-virgin olive oil
6 veal chops or steaks
1 large onion, sliced
1 garlic clove, crushed
1 (7-oz.) can chopped tomatoes
1 teaspoon tomato paste
Salt and pepper
1 teaspoon dried leaf oregano
1/2 teaspoon ground cinnamon
2/3 cup water
Toasted pine nuts and oregano sprigs, to garnish

In a skillet, heat olive oil. Add chops. Cook on one side until brown, then turn and brown other side. Transfer to a plate and keep warm.

Add onion and garlic to pan and cook a few minutes until soft. Stir in tomatoes, tomato paste, salt, pepper, oregano, cinnamon and water.

Return chops to pan. Spoon some of the sauce over them. Simmer, uncovered, 20 minutes, or until chops are cooked and sauce is thick. Sprinkle toasted pine nuts and oregano over the top before serving.

Makes 4 servings.

LEMON CHICKEN

1/4 cup butter
Grated zest and juice of 1 lemon
1 tablespoon chopped fresh oregano
1 (4-lb.) roasting chicken
1/2 cup chicken stock
Salt and pepper
Lemon slices and parsley sprigs, to garnish
SAUCE:
3 eggs
Juice of 1/2 lemon

Preheat oven to 350F (175C). Place half of butter, the lemon zest and most of oregano inside chicken.

Melt remaining butter in a large flameproof casserole dish. Add chicken and brown all over. Pour in lemon juice, stock, salt, pepper and remaining oregano. Cover casserole and roast 1-1/4 to 1-1/2 hours or until chicken is cooked and juices run clear when the thickest part is pierced. Transfer chicken to a heated dish. Measure 1 cup of the cooking liquid.

To make the sauce, in a bowl, whisk together eggs and lemon juice. Gradually whisk in hot cooking liquid. Place bowl over a pan of simmering water and heat gently, stirring, until sauce is thick and smooth. Add salt and pepper. Carve chicken and arrange on a hot serving plate. Pour the sauce over the chicken. Garnish with lemon and parsley.

Makes 6 servings.

— BROILED CHICKEN BREASTS —

1/4 cup extra-virgin olive oil
Juice of 1/2 lemon
1 tablespoon chopped fresh marjoram
1 tablespoon chopped fresh thyme
6 chicken breast halves
Cooked rice, to serve
Salt and pepper
Fresh thyme and marjoram sprigs and lemon peel strips,
   to garnish

In a shallow dish, mix together oil, lemon juice, marjoram and thyme.

Prick chicken flesh with a fork. Turn chicken pieces in marinade, then cover dish and refrigerate up to 8 hours.

Preheat broiler. Remove chicken from marinade and place, skin-side down, under broiler. Brush with marinade mixture and broil 8 to 10 minutes, basting occasionally with marinade. Turn chicken pieces over and broil 8 to 10 minutes or until golden-brown and cooked through. Stir pan juices into rice and season with salt and pepper. Serve chicken with the rice, garnished with thyme, marjoram and lemon peel.

Makes 6 servings.

KLEFTIKO

1 (3-lb.) chicken
1 lemon, quartered
2 teaspoons dried leaf oregano
Salt and pepper
2 tablespoons extra-virgin olive oil
1 red onion, thinly sliced
1/2 cup dry white wine
Lemon zest and oregano sprigs, to garnish

Preheat oven to 325F (165C). With a sharp knife, cut chicken into 4 quarters. Rub each chicken quarter all over with lemon.

In a bowl, mix together dried oregano, 1 teaspoon salt and pepper to taste. Rub mixture over each chicken quarter. Cut 4 squares of foil large enough to wrap around a chicken quarter. Brush foil with olive oil. Place a piece of chicken in the middle of each foil square. Scatter sliced onion over chicken. Pour 2 tablespoons wine over each piece of chicken.

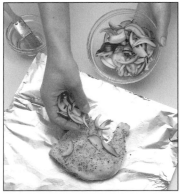

Seal edges of foil to make a package. Place packages on a baking sheet and bake in the oven 1 to 1-1/2 hours or until chicken is cooked and the juices run clear when the thickest part is pierced with a knife. To serve, open each package and slide contents onto a warmed plate. Garnish with lemon zest and oregano.

Makes 4 servings.

CHICKEN PIE

1 (3-1/4 to 3-1/2-lb.) roasting chicken
Chicken stock
3 cups sliced onions
2/3 cup milk
1/2 cup butter, melted
1 tablespoon fresh lemon juice
1 cup grated kefalotiri cheese (4 ounces)
Salt and pepper
1/4 teaspoon freshly grated nutmeg
1 tablespoon chopped fresh parsley
2 eggs, beaten
12 sheets filo pastry
Salad greens, to garnish

Into a flameproof casserole dish which the chicken fits tightly, put the chicken. Pour in enough stock to almost cover legs. Cover chicken breast with a sheet of buttered waxed paper. Cover and simmer 1 hour, or until chicken is just cooked. Remove chicken from casserole dish and cool.

Add onions and milk to stock. Boil rapidly, uncovered, until liquid is reduced to 1-1/4 cups of thick pulpy onion sauce. Preheat oven to 350F (175C).

Remove skin from chicken. Cut meat into small pieces and place in a large bowl. Add onion sauce, half the butter, the lemon juice, cheese, salt, pepper, nutmeg, parsley and eggs. Mix well together.

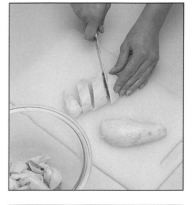

Lightly butter roasting pan. Brush 1 sheet of dough with butter and place in pan, overlapping edges. Brush 5 more sheets of dough with butter and layer them on top.

Spread the filling over the dough. Flap overlapping dough over top. Cut remaining sheets of dough to fit pan. Brush with butter and layer on top. Score top into squares and sprinkle with water. Bake 45 minutes, or until golden-brown and crisp. Serve with salad greens.

Makes 6 to 8 servings.

─── ROAST STUFFED POUSSIN ───

2 poussins, each weighing about 1-3/4 pounds
2 tablespoons butter for spreading
Salt and pepper
STUFFING:
1 ounce dried chestnuts
1/4 cup long-grain rice
1/4 cup shelled pistachio nuts
1/4 cup dried currants
Salt and pepper
1/2 teaspoon ground cinnamon
1/4 cup butter

To make the stuffing, in a bowl, put chest-nuts. Cover with cold water and let soak several hours.

Drain chestnuts, put into a saucepan and cover with cold water. Bring to a boil. Cover and simmer 20 to 30 minutes or until chest-nuts are tender. Drain and cool. Bring 1/2 cup of water to a boil. Add rice, cover and cook 8 to 10 minutes or until just tender. Preheat oven to 375F (190C). Chop chest-nuts and pistachio nuts finely. Put in a bowl with rice, currants, salt, pepper and cinna-mon. Mix well.

In a skillet, melt butter. Add stuffing mixture. Cook, stirring, until thoroughly combined. Allow to cool. Stuff poussins with stuffing. Spread a little butter over each bird. Season with salt and pepper. Place in a roast-ing pan and roast, basting occasionally, 45 minutes or until thoroughly cooked and golden-brown. Cut each poussin in half. Serve with the stuffing and pan juices.

Makes 4 servings.

—— GUINEA FOWL CASSEROLE ——

1/4 cup extra-virgin olive oil
1 guinea fowl, cut into 4 pieces
1 large onion, finely sliced
1 garlic clove, crushed
1 (14-oz.) can chopped tomatoes
1-1/4 cups water
1 tablespoon chopped fresh oregano
Salt and pepper
1 pound small okra
Halved ripe olives, to garnish

In a flameproof casserole dish, heat oil. Add guinea fowl pieces and cook on both sides until brown. Transfer to a plate.

Add onion and garlic to casserole dish and cook until soft. Add tomatoes, water, oregano, salt and pepper. Bring to a boil, then add guinea fowl and coat well with sauce. Cover pan and simmer 40 minutes.

Trim ends of okra without cutting pods. Put into a bowl of cold water and rinse gently, then pour into a strainer. Repeat until water is clear. Spread okra over guinea fowl. Cover and simmer 30 minutes or until okra is tender. Scatter ripe olives over the top and serve.

Makes 4 servings.

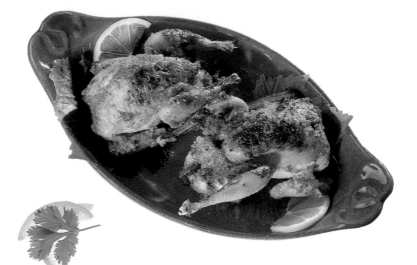

———— SPICY BROILED QUAIL ————

1 garlic clove
Salt
1 teaspoon each ground cumin and coriander
1/2 small onion, coarsely chopped
1 tablespoon chopped fresh cilantro
Pinch of red (cayenne) pepper
1/3 cup extra-virgin olive oil
8 quail
Grape leaves, parsley and lemon slices, to garnish

Into a food processor, put all the ingredients except quail and garnish.

Process to make a paste. Spread paste over quail. Cover and refrigerate 2 hours. Meanwhile, preheat broiler.

Broil quail 10 to 15 minutes, turning frequently, until cooked through and slightly charred on the outside. Serve quail on grape leaves, garnished with parsley and lemon slices.

Makes 4 servings.

Variation: Baby poussins or chicken portions can be cooked in this way.

Note: The quail are particularly good grilled on a barbecue.

────── POACHER'S PARTRIDGE ──────

1/2 lemon
2 young partridges
4 fresh thyme sprigs
4 fresh oregano sprigs
2 bay leaves
2 garlic cloves
Salt and pepper
6 bacon slices
Extra-virgin olive oil
Fresh herbs and lemon slices, to garnish
Fried potatoes, to serve

Preheat oven to 325F (165C). Rub lemon over partridges.

Put thyme, oregano, a bay leaf and a garlic clove in each bird. Season with salt and pepper. Wrap 3 bacon slices around each bird.

Brush 2 sheets of foil with oil. Wrap partridges in foil. Place packages in a roasting pan. Bake 1 hour or until partridges are tender and juices run clear when the thickest part is pierced with a knife. Cut each partridge in half. Serve with the cooking juices poured over them, garnished with herbs and lemon slices and accompanied by fried potatoes.

Makes 4 servings.

RABBIT STIFADO

2 tablespoons all-purpose flour
Salt and pepper
1-1/2 to 2 pounds rabbit pieces
1/3 cup extra-virgin olive oil
1 pound tiny pearl onions
1 garlic clove, crushed
1 tablespoon tomato paste
1-1/4 cups red wine
1-1/4 cups chicken stock
1 bay leaf
2 fresh thyme sprigs
2 bread slices, crusts removed
2 tablespoons chopped fresh parsley

On a plate, mix together flour, salt and pepper. Toss rabbit pieces in seasoned flour. In a skillet, heat half the oil. Fry rabbit pieces until brown on both sides. Transfer to a flameproof casserole dish. Add onions to skillet and cook until they begin to brown. Add garlic and tomato paste to pan, then stir in wine and stock. Add bay leaf, thyme, salt and pepper. Add to casserole dish, cover and cook over low heat 1-1/2 to 2 hours or until rabbit is tender.

Cut each slice of bread into 4 triangles. In a skillet, heat remaining oil. Fry bread until golden-brown on both sides. Dip one edge of each triangle into chopped parsley. To serve, place rabbit on a shallow plate and arrange onions around edge. Pour the sauce over the rabbit and garnish with fried bread.

Makes 6 servings.

PITA BREAD

7 cups bread flour
1 envelope active dry yeast (about 1 tablespoon)
2 teaspoons salt
2 tablespoons extra-virgin olive oil

Into a large bowl, sift flour. Stir in yeast and salt. Add oil and mix in enough water to make a soft dough. Turn dough out onto a floured surface.

Knead dough thoroughly 10 minutes or until smooth and elastic. Cut into 12 equal-size pieces. Roll each piece into a ball, then roll out to an oval shape 7 inches long. Place on floured trays, cover with a cloth and leave in a warm place 1 hour or until doubled in size.

Preheat oven to 475F (240C). Oil 2 baking sheets and place in the oven to heat. Place 3 pita breads on each baking sheet and sprinkle with water. Bake 5 minutes or until puffed and lightly browned. Remove from baking sheets and wrap in a cloth while baking remaining bread.

Makes 12.

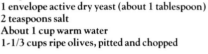

OLIVE BREAD

1/3 cup extra-virgin olive oil
1 onion, finely chopped
7 cups bread flour
1 envelope active dry yeast (about 1 tablespoon)
2 teaspoons salt
About 1 cup warm water
1-1/3 cups ripe olives, pitted and chopped

In a skillet, heat oil. Add onion and cook until soft. Let cool. Into a large bowl, sift flour. Stir in yeast and salt. Add 2 tablespoons of the cooking oil and mix in enough water to make a soft dough. Turn dough out onto a floured surface.

Knead dough thoroughly 10 minutes or until smooth and elastic. Knead in 1 tablespoon of the cooking oil, the fried onion, reserving remaining oil, and chopped olives. Cut dough in half and shape into 2 round loaves. Place on lightly oiled baking sheets.

Cover with oiled plastic wrap and leave in a warm place 1 hour, or until doubled in size. Preheat oven to 350F (175C). Brush loaves with a little of the cooking oil. Bake loaves 30 to 40 minutes or until bottom of each sounds hollow when tapped. Brush tops of loaves with remaining oil. Return to the oven 2 minutes, then transfer to wire racks to cool.

Makes 2 loaves.

CHEESE BUNS

7 cups bread flour
1 envelope active dry yeast (about 1 tablespoon)
2 teaspoons salt
2 teaspoons sugar
2 tablespoons extra-virgin olive oil
About 2 cups warm water
Sesame seeds, to garnish
CHEESE FILLING:
12 ounces kefalotiri cheese, grated
4 ounces haloumi cheese, finely chopped
1 tablespoon all-purpose flour
1 teaspoon baking powder
1 tablespoon chopped fresh mint
1/4 teaspoon freshly grated nutmeg
4 eggs, beaten

To make the filling, into a bowl, put cheeses. Add flour, baking powder, mint and nutmeg to cheese. Stir in most of beaten egg, reserving extra egg, to make a stiff paste. To make the dough, into a bowl, sift flour. Stir in yeast, salt and sugar. Add oil and mix in enough warm to make a soft dough. Turn dough out onto a floured surface and knead 10 minutes or until smooth and elastic. Divide into 16 pieces; roll out each piece to a 4-inch circle.

Place a little filling in center of each circle. Pull dough up on 3 sides to make a triangular shape, with filling showing in center. Pinch corners together well. Place on oiled baking sheets, cover with oiled plastic wrap and leave in a warm place until doubled in size. Preheat oven to 450F (225C). Brush buns with remaining beaten egg. Sprinkle with sesame seeds. Bake 12 to 15 minutes or until golden-brown.

Makes 16.

EASTER BREAD

7 cups bread flour
1 envelope active dry yeast (about 1 tablespoon)
1/4 cup superfine sugar
2 teaspoons caraway seeds
1/2 cup butter, melted
2 eggs, beaten
1 cup warm milk
1 egg, beaten, for glazing
2 tablespoons slivered almonds, to decorate

Into a large bowl, sift flour. Stir in yeast, sugar and caraway seeds. Stir in butter, eggs and milk. Mix together, then turn dough out onto a floured surface.

Knead dough thoroughly 10 minutes or until smooth and elastic. Cut dough in half and divide each half into 3 pieces. Roll each piece into a rope 20 inches long. Braid 3 ropes, then shape the braid into a ring, pressing the ends together firmly. Braid remaining 3 ropes. Place the 2 rings on oiled baking sheets. Cover with a cloth and leave in a warm place 1 hour or until doubled in size. Preheat oven to 375F (190C).

Brush loaves with beaten egg. Scatter slivered almonds over the top. Bake 40 minutes or until loaves are lightly browned and sound hollow when tapped on the bottoms. Leave on wire racks to cool. Serve sliced and buttered.

Makes 2 loaves.

Note: Traditionally these loaves have red-dyed eggs tucked into the braids before baking.

EASTER COOKIES

2/3 cup walnuts
1/2 cup sunflower oil
1/2 cup superfine sugar
2 tablespoons dried currants
1 egg
1-1/2 cups all-purpose flour
1 teaspoon baking powder
1/4 teaspoon vanilla extract
Powdered sugar

Preheat oven to 350F (175C). Grease 2 baking sheets. In a food processor, chop walnuts finely. In a bowl, mix together walnuts, sunflower oil, sugar, currants and egg.

Sift in flour and baking powder. Add vanilla extract. Stir together to form a firm paste, adding more flour if too soft.

Roll mixture into small walnut-size balls, flatten slightly and place on prepared baking sheets. Bake 10 minutes, or until crisp and golden. Transfer to wire racks to cool. Dust with powdered sugar as they cool.

Makes about 14.

FESTIVAL CRESCENTS

4-1/2 ounces hazelnuts
1-1/4 cups unsalted butter, softened
1/4 cup superfine sugar
1 egg yolk
2 tablespoons brandy
1/2 cup cornstarch
2-1/2 cups all-purpose flour
Orange-flower water
Powdered sugar

In a food processor, chop nuts finely, without reducing to ground hazelnuts. Preheat oven to 350F (175C). Butter 2 or 3 baking sheets.

In a bowl, cream butter and superfine sugar until pale and fluffy. Beat in egg yolk and brandy. Stir in hazelnuts. Sift cornstarch and flour over mixture. Stir in, adding more flour, if necessary, to make a firm dough. With floured hands, break off small pieces of dough and roll into 3-inch pieces, tapering into pointed ends. Shape into crescents; place on baking sheets. Bake 20 to 25 minutes or until firm. Reduce heat if cookies brown. Transfer to wire racks to cool.

Into a small bowl, pour orange-flower water. Into a large bowl, put powdered sugar. Dip crescents very briefly into orange-flower water, then into powdered sugar, to coat completely. Pack loosely in a pan to avoid cookies sticking together.

Makes about 40.

VANILLA RINGS

1/2 cup butter, softened
1/3 cup superfine sugar
1/2 teaspoon vanilla extract
1 egg yolk
1-1/2 cups all-purpose flour
1/2 teaspoon baking powder
1-1/2 teaspoons ouzo
2 tablespoons chopped blanched almonds

Preheat oven to 350F (175C). Grease 2 baking sheets. In a bowl, cream together butter and sugar until light and fluffy.

Beat in vanilla extract and egg yolk. Sift flour and baking powder over mixture, then add ouzo and mix to a smooth dough. Break off walnut-size pieces of dough.

Roll the pieces into short ropes and join the ends to make rings. Place on prepared baking sheets and sprinkle chopped almonds over the rings. Bake 5 to 20 minutes or until pale gold. Transfer to wire racks to cool.

Makes about 16.

APRICOPITA

2 pounds fresh apricots
Seeds from 5 cardamom pods
1/2 cup superfine sugar
1/4 teaspoon vanilla extract
6 tablespoons butter, melted
12 sheets filo pastry
3 egg whites
3 tablespoons light brown sugar
1-1/4 cups ground blanched almonds
Powdered sugar

Into a bowl, put apricots. Cover with boiling water and leave 2 minutes, then drain. Cover with cold water, leave 2 minutes and drain again.

Peel skins off apricots. Cut in half and remove pits. Put apricots in a saucepan with cardamom seeds, superfine sugar and vanilla extract. Cook gently until apricots are soft. In a blender or food processor fitted with the metal blade, puree the apricots. Preheat oven to 375F (190C). Brush a 13" x 9" baking pan with melted butter. Brush a sheet of dough with butter and lay it in pan. Repeat with 3 more sheets. Spread apricot puree on top. Cover with 4 more layers of buttered dough sheets.

In a bowl, whisk egg whites until stiff but not dry. Whisk in brown sugar. Fold in ground almonds. Spread meringue on dough. Cover gently with 4 more sheets of buttered dough. Tuck top layer of dough down sides. With a sharp knife, cut diamond shapes in dough, down to meringue layer. Dust with powdered sugar, then bake 40 to 50 minutes or until browned and crisp. Serve warm or cold, cut into diamonds, and dusted with more sugar.

Makes 6 to 8 servings.

BAKLAVA

1 cup blanched almonds
1 cup walnuts
1/3 cup pistachio nuts
1/3 cup packed brown sugar
1 teaspoon ground cinnamon
1/4 teaspoon freshly grated nutmeg
1/4 cup butter
8 sheets filo pastry
SYRUP:
1 cup granulated sugar
2/3 cup water
1 tablespoon fresh lemon juice
1 tablespoon orange-flower water

To make syrup, in a saucepan, heat sugar, water and lemon juice until sugar dissolves. Boil gently 5 minutes or until syrupy. Add orange-flower water and boil 2 minutes. Cool completely. In a food processor fitted with the metal blade, process one-third of all nuts until finely chopped. Coarsely chop remaining nuts. In a bowl, mix together nuts, brown sugar, cinnamon and nutmeg. Butter a 13" x 9" baking pan. Preheat oven to 350F (175C). In a saucepan, melt butter.

Cut dough sheets in half across. Brush one halved sheet with butter and place on bottom of roasting pan. Repeat with 3 more sheets. Spread one-third of nut mixture over the top, then repeat the layers twice more, ending with a layer of dough. With a sharp knife, cut top layer of dough into diamonds. Bake in oven 30 to 40 minutes until crisp and golden. Pour cold syrup over the top. When cold, trim edges and cut into diamond shapes.

Makes about 20.

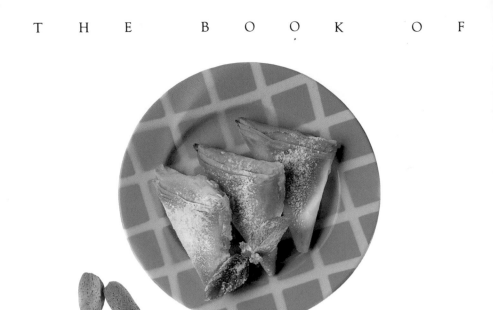

— CHEESE & HONEY TRIANGLES —

**1 (8-oz.) package cream cheese, softened
2 tablespoons creamed honey
1 egg yolk
1/4 cup butter
6 sheets filo pastry
Powdered sugar for dusting**

Preheat oven to 375F (190C). Butter a baking sheet. In a bowl, beat together cream cheese, honey and egg yolk.

In a small saucepan, melt butter. Brush a sheet of filo dough with melted butter. Cover with a second sheet of dough and brush with butter. Cover with a third sheet of dough. Cut dough layers in half across. Cut each half crosswise into 4 strips. Repeat with remaining 3 sheets of dough.

Place a spoonful of cream cheese mixture on corner of a filo dough strip. Fold dough and filling over at right angles to make a triangle and continue folding in this way along strip of dough to form a neat triangular package. Place on baking sheet and brush with melted butter. Repeat with remaining dough strips and filling. Bake 10 minutes until crisp. Dust lightly with powdered sugar.

Makes 16.

WALNUT PASTRIES

2-1/2 cups all-purpose flour
3/4 cup butter, chilled
1/3 cup powdered sugar
1 egg yolk
3 tablespoons superfine sugar
1/3 cup water
1 cup coarsely chopped walnuts
1/2 cup chopped mixed citrus peel
1/4 teaspoon freshly grated nutmeg
3 tablespoons rosewater
Extra powdered sugar for coating

Into a bowl, sift flour. Cut in butter until mixture resembles bread crumbs.

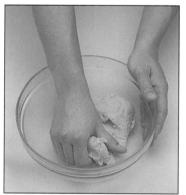

Sift powdered sugar over flour mixture. Stir in powdered sugar, egg yolk and a little water to make a firm dough. Cover and refrigerate 30 minutes. Preheat oven to 350F (175C). Butter a baking sheet. To make the syrup, in a saucepan, put superfine sugar and the water. Heat over low heat until sugar has dissolved. Bring to a boil and boil a few minutes until syrup has reduced and thickened slightly.

In a bowl, mix together walnuts, citrus peel and nutmeg. Stir in syrup. On a floured surface, thinly roll out pastry. Cut out 4-inch circles. Place a teaspoon of walnut mixture on each circle. Fold in half, pressing edges together. Bake in the oven 20 to 30 minutes until pale golden. Brush with rosewater. Coat liberally with powdered sugar.

Makes about 20.

CINNAMON KNOTS

1 cup all-purpose flour
1/2 teaspoon baking powder
2 tablespoons sunflower oil
2 eggs, beaten
Grated zest of 1/2 orange
Sunflower oil for deep-frying
3 tablespoons honey
Chopped walnuts and ground cinnamon, to decorate

Into a bowl, sift flour and baking powder. Stir in oil, eggs and orange zest. Mix to a firm dough, adding more flour if necessary. Cover and refrigerate 30 minutes.

On a floured surface, thinly roll out dough. With a pastry wheel, cut into 5″ x 1″ strips. Carefully tie into knots. Heat oil in a deep-fryer and deep-fry the knots, a few at a time. Drain on paper towels, then pile onto a serving dish.

In a small pan, heat honey. Pour it over knots and sprinkle with walnuts and cinnamon.

Makes about 24.

KADAIFI

1 cup finely chopped walnuts
1 cup finely chopped almonds
1/4 cup superfine sugar
1/2 teaspoon ground cinnamon
14 ounces kadaifi pastry dough (see Note)
1/4 cup butter
SYRUP:
1 cup granulated sugar
1-1/4 cups water
1 tablespoon fresh lemon juice
1 tablespoon orange-flower water

Preheat oven to 350F (175C). Butter a 13" x 9" baking pan. In a bowl, mix together walnuts, almonds, sugar and cinnamon.

Tease dough out to an 18" x 15" rectangle. Cut into 18 pieces, each 5" x 3". Place 1 tablespoon of nut mixture on short end of each rectangle of dough. Roll up, enclosing filling. Place rolls in prepared pan. In a small saucepan, melt butter, then pour it over the rolls. Bake 25 to 30 minutes or until golden and crisp. Cool 15 minutes.

To make the syrup, put sugar, water and lemon juice in a saucepan. Heat gently until sugar has dissolved, then boil 5 minutes or until slightly thickened. Add orange-flower water, then pour syrup over pastry rolls.

Makes 18.

Note: Kadaifi is a white shredded raw pastry dough available from delicatessens and Greek specialty stores. It has to be teased into shape rather than rolled.

HONEY CAKES

2 cups all-purpose flour
1/2 teaspoon ground cinnamon
1/4 teaspoon ground cloves
1/4 teaspoon freshly grated nutmeg
1/4 cup superfine sugar
2 tablespoons dry white wine
2 tablespoons ouzo
Juice of 1/2 orange
1 tablespoon brandy
1/2 cup sunflower oil
Chopped almonds and ground cinnamon, to decorate
SYRUP:
1/2 cup honey
1/2 cup superfine sugar
1/2 cup water
2 tablespoons fresh lemon juice

Preheat oven to 400F (205C). Grease a baking sheet. Into a bowl, sift flour, cinnamon, cloves and nutmeg. Stir in sugar. In another bowl, mix together wine, ouzo, orange juice and brandy. Stir oil into flour, then gradually beat in other liquid mixture until a stiff dough is formed. Add more flour if necessary. Break off pieces the size of a large walnut. Form into balls, place on baking sheet and press to flatten slightly. Bake 15 minutes or until brown.

Meanwhile, make the syrup. In a saucepan, put honey, sugar, water and lemon juice. Heat gently until sugar is dissolved. Bring to a boil and boil until mixture is frothy. While cakes are still warm, soak them in syrup 2 minutes. Place on wire racks. Sprinkle with almonds, then cinnamon.

Makes about 14.

HALVA CAKE

1/2 cup butter
1/2 cup superfine sugar
Grated zest of 1 orange
Juice of 1/2 lemon
2 eggs, beaten
1 cup semolina
2 teaspoons baking powder
1 cup ground blanched almonds
1 teaspoon ground cinnamon
SYRUP:
3/4 cup superfine sugar
Juice of 1/2 lemon
Juice of 1/2 orange
1/2 cup water
2 tablespoons candied orange peel, to decorate

Preheat oven to 425C (220C). Butter a ring mold. In a food processor fitted with the metal blade, put butter, sugar, orange zest, juice, eggs, semolina, baking powder, ground almonds and cinnamon. Process until well mixed. Turn mixture into prepared mold. Bake 10 minutes, then reduce heat to 350F (175C) and bake 25 minutes, or until a wooden pick inserted into cake comes out clean. Cool in the mold a few minutes, then turn out into a warm, deep plate.

Meanwhile, make the syrup. Into a pan, put sugar, lemon juice, orange juice and the water. Heat gently until sugar has dissolved, then bring to a boil and simmer 4 minutes. Stir in candied peel. As soon as cake is turned out, bring syrup to the boil, then spoon over cake so peel is arranged decoratively over the cake.

Makes 8 servings.

ARTEMIS CAKE

14 ounces semisweet chocolate
5 eggs, separated
1 cup butter, softened
3/4 cup powdered sugar, sifted
2 tablespoons all-purpose flour, sifted
1 teaspoon ground cinnamon
Extra powdered sugar, to decorate

Preheat oven to 350C (175C). Butter and line an 8-inch cake pan with waxed paper (preferably a loose-bottomed pan). Into a bowl, break chocolate. Stand bowl over a pan of hot water until melted. Leave until almost cold.

In a bowl, whisk egg whites until stiff but not dry. In another bowl, beat butter and powdered sugar until light and creamy. Beat in egg yolks. Stir in chocolate. It does not need to be thoroughly mixed.

Stir in flour and cinnamon, then fold in egg whites. Pour mixture into prepared pan. Bake 45 minutes or until firm to the touch. Leave in pan until almost cool, then transfer to a wire rack. Sift powdered sugar over the top and place on a serving plate.

Makes 8 servings.

YOGURT CAKE

4 eggs, separated
1-1/2 cups sugar
1/2 cup sunflower oil
1/4 teaspoon baking soda
1 cup plain yogurt
Grated zest of 1 lemon
2-1/2 cups all-purpose flour
1 tablespoon baking powder
Powdered sugar

Preheat oven to 375F (190C). Grease and line a 9-inch round cake pan. In a bowl, whisk egg yolks and sugar until creamy.

Gradually mix in oil. Stir baking soda into yogurt. Stir yogurt and half the lemon zest into egg yolk mixture. Sift flour and baking powder into mixture and fold in carefully. Beat egg whites until stiff but not dry, then fold into batter.

Pour mixture into prepared pan. Bake 40 to 50 minutes or until a wooden pick inserted into the center comes out clean. Leave in pan 5 minutes, then transfer to a wire rack to cool. Dust with powdered sugar and sprinkle remaining lemon zest over the top.

Makes 8 to 10 servings.

LAVENDER & HONEY ICE CREAM

5 sprigs lavender flowers
2-1/2 cups milk
3/4 cup lavender honey
4 egg yolks
2/3 cup whipping cream
2/3 cup plain yogurt
Lavender flowers, to decorate

Turn freezer to its coldest setting. In a saucepan, heat lavender sprigs and milk to almost boiling. Remove from heat and leave to infuse 30 minutes. Remove lavender sprigs and bring milk back to a boil.

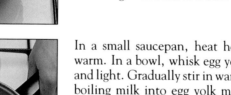

In a small saucepan, heat honey until just warm. In a bowl, whisk egg yolks until thick and light. Gradually stir in warm honey. Pour boiling milk into egg yolk mixture, beating constantly. Pour mixture into a bowl set over a pan of simmering water. Stir about 8 minutes or until custard will coat the back of the spoon. Strain into a bowl, cover and refrigerate until cool. Stir in cream and yogurt.

Pour mixture into a 3-3/4-cup freezerproof container. Put in freezer. When sides are beginning to set, beat thoroughly. Return to freezer and repeat after 30 to 40 minutes. When ice cream is just beginning to solidify, beat vigorously to a smooth slush. Return to freezer. Transfer from freezer to refrigerator 20 minutes before serving. Decorate with lavender flowers.

Makes 4 to 6 servings.

– PISTACHIO HALVA ICE CREAM –

3 egg yolks
1/2 cup superfine sugar
1-1/4 cups half and half
1-1/4 cups whipping cream
4 ounces pistachio halva
Chopped pistachio nuts, to decorate

Turn freezer to its lowest setting. In a bowl, whisk together egg yolks and sugar until thick and pale. In a small saucepan, bring half and half to a boil, then pour onto egg yolk mixture and mix well.

Transfer to double boiler or heatproof bowl placed over a pan of simmering water. Cook, stirring constantly, until custard will coat the back of the spoon. Strain into a bowl, cover and refrigerate until cool. In a bowl, whip cream lightly, then whisk into custard. Crumble halva into mixture and stir in gently.

Pour into a freezerproof container. Cover and freeze 3 hours or until half frozen. Stir well, then return to freezer until frozen. Remove from freezer 15 minutes before serving. Decorate with chopped pistachio nuts.

Makes 6 servings.

DRIED FRUIT SALAD

3/4 cup packed light brown sugar
2/3 cup warm water
2 tablespoons rosewater
2 cups cold water
1/2 pound dried apricots
1/2 pound dates
1/2 pound dried figs
3/4 cup raisins
3/4 cup slivered blanched almonds
1/4 cup pistachio nuts
Yogurt, to serve

In a bowl, put sugar and warm water. Stir until sugar has dissolved. Stir in rosewater and cold water. Add apricots, dates, figs and raisins to bowl. Stir and turn them in the liquid, adding more water, if necessary, to cover.

Cover bowl and refrigerate at least 24 hours. When ready to serve, add almonds and pistachio nuts and stir to mix with the fruit. Serve with yogurt.

Makes 6 to 8 servings.

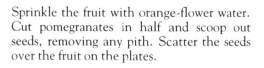

FRUIT PLATTER

1 small melon
2 peaches
4 figs
6 ounces seedless green grapes
Orange-flower water
2 pomegranates

With a sharp knife, halve melon and remove and discard seeds. Cut into thin slices and remove skin. Arrange slices on 4 plates.

Into a bowl, put peaches and pour boiling water over them. Leave 30 seconds, then plunge into cold water 30 seconds. Peel off skins. Cut peaches in half and remove and discard pits. Cut into slices and arrange on the plates. Cut figs into slices and add to the plates. Arrange grapes on the plates.

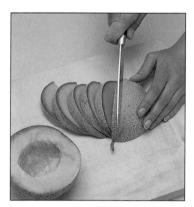

Sprinkle the fruit with orange-flower water. Cut pomegranates in half and scoop out seeds, removing any pith. Scatter the seeds over the fruit on the plates.

Makes 4 servings.

CUSTARD PASTRIES

2 eggs, separated
1/2 cup superfine sugar
1/3 cup semolina
2-1/2 cups milk
6 tablespoons butter
8 sheets filo pastry
Powdered sugar and ground cinnamon, to decorate

In a bowl, beat together egg yolks, sugar, semolina and a little of the milk until creamy.

In a saucepan, heat remaining milk until almost boiling. Gradually whisk milk into egg mixture. Return to saucepan. Cook gently, stirring, 5 minutes or until mixture thickens. Stir in 1 tablespoon of the butter. Cover surface closely with plastic wrap. Refrigerate until cold. In a bowl, whisk egg whites until stiff but not dry. Fold into custard. Preheat oven to 400F (205C). Butter a baking sheet.

In a small pan, melt remaining butter. Brush a sheet of dough with butter. Place another sheet on top; brush with butter. Repeat with 2 more sheets. Cut pastry dough into 12 squares. Put a little custard mixture in middle of each square. Draw edges of dough together to form a pouch. Pinch neck firmly together. Repeat with remaining pastry and filling. Place pastries on baking sheets. Bake 15 minutes or until golden-brown. Dust with powdered sugar and cinnamon.

Makes 24.

HONEY CHEESECAKES

1 tablespoon raisins
1 tablespoon orange-flower water
1 (8-oz.) package cream cheese, softened
3 tablespoons orange-blossom honey
2 small eggs, beaten
Fresh mint leaves, to decorate
PASTRY:
1-1/4 cups all-purpose flour
6 tablespoons butter
3 tablespoons powdered sugar
1 egg yolk
CANDIED ORANGE PEEL:
1/2 cup superfine sugar
1/3 cup water
1 ounce orange peel, cut into julienne strips

Put raisins and orange-flower water in a small bowl to soak. To make the pastry, sift flour into a bowl. Cut in butter until mixture resembles bread crumbs. Stir in powdered sugar. Mix in egg yolk and a little water to make a firm dough. Cover and refrigerate 30 minutes. To make the candied orange peel, put sugar and the water into a saucepan. Heat gently until sugar is dissolved. Bring to a boil and boil 2 minutes. Blanch orange peel 2 to 3 minutes in boiling water. Drain, add to syrup and cook 20 minutes or until peel is transparent.

Preheat oven to 350F (175C). On a floured surface, thinly roll dough out. Use to line 4 deep loose-bottom 4-inch tart pans. In a bowl, beat together raisins, cream cheese, honey and eggs. Pour into pastry shells. Bake 25 to 30 minutes or until set and golden. Decorate with orange peel and mint leaves.

Makes 4.

RIZOGALO

1/2 cup rice
1/2 cup water
2-1/2 cups milk
1 piece of lemon zest
1/4 cup superfine sugar
1-1/2 teaspoons cornstarch
1 egg yolk, beaten
2 teaspoons rosewater
Ground cinnamon and rose petals, to decorate
  (optional)

Rinse rice. Put in a bowl with the water.

In a saucepan, put milk and lemon zest, then bring to a boil. Add sugar and stir until dissolved. Add the rice and water. Simmer, covered, 30 to 40 minutes or until most of the milk has been absorbed.

Mix cornstarch with a little water, add to rice and cook 2 to 3 minutes, stirring. Stir in egg yolk and simmer 2 to 3 minutes, stirring. Stir in rosewater. Pour into serving dishes and cool. Decorate with ground cinnamon, then scatter rose petals over the top, if desired.

Makes 4 servings.

ORANGES & WALNUTS

4 oranges
1 teaspoon orange-flower water
4 ounces dates
2/3 cup walnuts
Fresh mint leaves, to decorate

With a sharp knife, carefully cut skins off oranges, removing any pith. Cut oranges into sections by cutting down between the membranes. Reserve any juice.

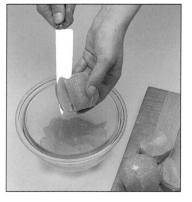

Arrange the sections on a serving plate. Pour reserved juice over the top and then sprinkle with orange-flower water.

Remove pits from dates. Chop dates and walnuts. Sprinkle them over the oranges. Serve decorated with mint leaves.

Makes 4 servings.

INDEX

Afelia, 80
Apricopita, 102
Artemis Cake, 110
Avgolemono Soup, 44

Baked Gray Mullet, 72
Baked Lamb with Vegetables, 77
Baklava, 103
Bean Dip, 24
Bean Soup, 46
Beans & Greens, 57
Black-Eyed Peas & Rice, 58
Broiled Chicken Breasts, 86
Broiled Mussels, 36
Broiled Sardines, 70
Broiled Vegetables, 28

Cheese & Herb Triangles, 12
Cheese & Honey Triangles, 104
Cheese Buns, 97
Chicken Pie, 88
Cinnamon Knots, 106
Coriander Mushrooms, 27
Country Salad, 51
Cucumber & Tomato Salad, 48
Cucumber & Yogurt Soup, 43
Custard Pastries, 116

Dolmades, 32
Dried Fruit Salad, 114

Easter Bread, 98
Easter Cookies, 99
Eggplant Salad, 18

Fasoulia, 59
Fava Beans & Artichokes, 55
Fava Beans with Dill, 56
Festival Crescents, 100
Fish Plaki, 65
Fisherman's Soup, 45

Fried Eggplant, 30
Fried Fish with Skordalia, 66
Fried Haloumi Salad, 20
Fried Squid, 34
Fruit Platter, 115

Garlic-Pepper Salad, 22
Grape Leaf-Wrapped Cheese, 16
Green Beans with Onion, 54
Ground Meat Pastries, 39
Guinea Fowl Casserole, 91

Halva Cake, 109
Herb & Feta Balls, 14
Honey Cakes, 108
Honey Cheesecakes, 117

Iman Bayaldi, 17

Kadaifi, 107
Keftedes, 40
Kleftiko, 87

Lamb Pastries, 76
Lamb Steaks with Pasta, 75
Lavender & Honey Ice Cream, 112
Leeks a la Grecque, 29
Lemon Chicken, 85
Lentil & Tomato Soup, 47
Lentil Salad, 53

Marinated Feta Cheese, 13
Marinated Olives, 23
Meatballs in Tomato Sauce, 38
Moussaka, 74

Okra & Tomatoes, 64
Olive Bread, 96
Oranges & Walnuts, 119

Pastitsio, 82
Pistachio Halva Ice Cream, 113

Pita Bread, 95
Poacher's Partridge, 93
Pork Kabobs, 41
Pork with Pears, 79
Potato Kephtedes, 61
Pourgouri Pilaf, 60

Rabbit Stifado, 94
Rizogalo, 118
Roast Stuffed Poussin, 90

Seafood Parcels, 35
Shrimp & Feta Tarts, 68
Shrimp & Saffron Sauce, 67
Snow Pea Salad, 52
Sofrito, 83
Souvlakia, 42
Spanakopitta, 15
Spiced Rack of Lamb, 78
Spicy Braised Beef, 81
Spicy Broiled Quail, 92
Spinach & Rice, 62
Squid & Shrimp Kabobs, 69
Squid Salad, 49
Squid with Red Wine, 71
Stuffed Eggplant, 73
Stuffed Tomatoes, 26
Stuffed Zucchini Rings, 31
Swordfish Kabobs, 37

Taramasalata, 33
Three Bean Salad, 50
Tomato Salad, 21
Tzatziki, 25

Vanilla Rings, 101
Veal Chops with Tomatoes, 84

Walnut Pastries, 105

Yogurt Cake, 111

Zucchini Salad, 19
Zucchini with Cheese, 63